Iron Age and Roman Wychwood

Other titles by Tim Copeland include

Mathematics and the Historic Environment (English Heritage, 1992)
Geography and the Historic Environment (English Heritage, 1993)
Castles and the Historic Environment (English Heritage, 1994)
The Ancient Greeks (Cambridge University Press, 1997)
A Teacher's Handbook for Local Studies (RCHM, 1998)
Investigating the Romans (National Trust, 2000)

Iron Age and Roman Wychwood

The Land of Satavacus and Bellicia

Tim Copeland

THE WYCHWOOD PRESS

Our books may be ordered from bookshops or (post free) from
Jon Carpenter Publishing, Alder House, Market Street, Charlbury, OX7 3PH
01608 811969

e-mail: wychwood@joncarpenter.co.uk

Credit card orders should be phoned or faxed to 01689 870437 or 01608 811969

Please ask for our free catalogue

First published in 2002 by
The Wychwood Press
an imprint of Jon Carpenter Publishing
Alder House, Market Street, Charlbury, Oxfordshire OX7 3PH

ISBN 1 902279 14 X

Printed in England by J. W. Arrowsmith Ltd., Bristol

Contents

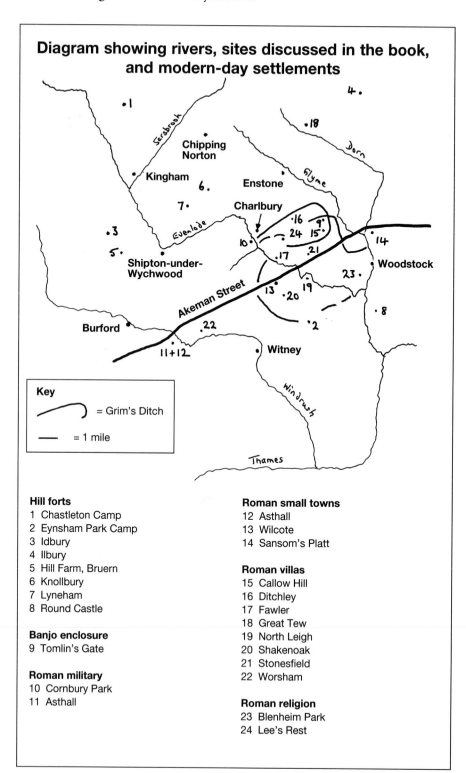

Diagram showing rivers, sites discussed in the book, and modern-day settlements

Chipping Norton

Kingham

Enstone

Charlbury

Shipton-under-Wychwood

Woodstock

Akeman Street

Burford

Witney

Key

= Grim's Ditch

= 1 mile

Hill forts
1 Chastleton Camp
2 Eynsham Park Camp
3 Idbury
4 Ilbury
5 Hill Farm, Bruern
6 Knollbury
7 Lyneham
8 Round Castle

Banjo enclosure
9 Tomlin's Gate

Roman military
10 Cornbury Park
11 Asthall

Roman small towns
12 Asthall
13 Wilcote
14 Sansom's Platt

Roman villas
15 Callow Hill
16 Ditchley
17 Fawler
18 Great Tew
19 North Leigh
20 Shakenoak
21 Stonesfield
22 Worsham

Roman religion
23 Blenheim Park
24 Lee's Rest

Introduction

One day, in the early centuries of the present era, two individuals carved their names on a pottery syrinx, a set of clay pipes. The pipes illustrated on the next page (Brodribb, Hands and Walker) were subsequently found in the excavation of Shakenoak Roman villa in the 1960s and though damaged, a male name, SATAVACUS , was quite clear. Unfortunately the second name had been truncated by a break but reads BELLICIA…, and belongs to a female. What is significant is that, besides possibly identifying a lover and his lass, these names are both from the pre-Roman Iron Age tradition even though the pipes were found in the debris of a building that was dated to almost two hundred years after the Roman invasion. The names on the pipes demonstrate continuity between the people living in Wychwood before the arrival of the Romans and those who worked the land for centuries after that event.

The Iron Age and Roman periods in Wychwood still have an impact on the area today. The pattern of the roads, the parish boundaries, the sites of villages and the distribution of vegetation have evolved in part from decisions taken to meet the inhabitants' needs in the period 800 BC to 400 AD. To some extent all of us who are lucky to live in the area experience the results of those decisions every day. Our routes to work, our leisurely footpath walks, even some of the names of the places we walk to, may have originated in that far-off period.

This book is about the evidence, or lack of it, in Wychwood for the Iron Age and Roman periods. It is also about the evolution of our understanding of that period of the past. The book examines the work of significant individuals who have constructed a dynamic past characterised by increasing knowledge and reflecting the concerns of the periods in which their explorations took place.

The book could not have been written without the help of many people over the last twenty years. Access to information and evidence has been facilitated by the Ditchley Estate, especially Robert Hobill and Chris Eaton, and Ival Hornbrook and Elizabeth Leggatt of the Oxfordshire Sites and Monuments Record. I benefited from discussion with James Bond, Hugh Coddington, Barry Cunliffe, Martin Henig, the late Lois Hey, Paul Jeffrey, George Lambrick, David Miles, Roy Townsend and Bob Wilkins. Birgit Holtz provided valuable support and encouragement through the process of writing. Any errors of fact are mine, not theirs. I hope that I have done justice to the many archaeologists who have worked in Wychwood in the past and whose material I have re-interpreted. Perhaps this book should be entitled 'Tim Copeland's Iron Age and Roman Wychwood' as it is, inevitably, a personal interpretation of the evidence and of other people's constructions of the past.

This book is for Anne, Emily and Tomos, who never begrudged the time I spent exploring the landscape and often, as Dylan Thomas would have said, 'airing my devils' in it. It is dedicated to SATAVACUS and BELLICIA of the subtitle, who could never in their wildest dreams have imagined that their identities would have survived in this way.

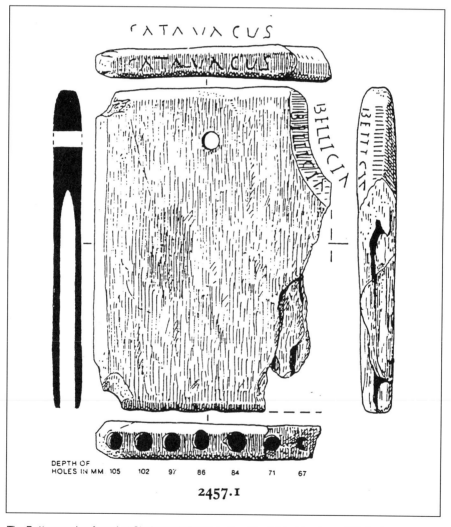

The Pottery syrinx found at Shakenoak Roman villa. (Brodribb, Hands and Walker)

1

Wychwood: The Physical Environment

When and where was Iron Age and Roman 'Wychwood'? The terms 'Iron Age' and 'Roman' immediately bring certain images to mind. On a simple timeline they identify the periods from when iron first began to be commonly used to the period of the Roman occupation. However, nothing is that simple in the past. On a more complex timeline which took into account the beliefs of the population, agricultural practice and types of building structure, there would be a lot of overlap between the periods and certainly with the preceding Bronze Age and the succeeding sub-Roman period. Chronologies are constructed to identify change. The changes identified by the terms 'Iron Age' and 'Roman' were not as sudden as perhaps was once thought. Even the dates that we assign to the Iron Age (800 BC–43 AD) are arbitrary for Wychwood. At the beginning of the period it is likely that flint, bronze and iron were in use at a variety of social levels and by the end, although the Roman army had begun its invasion, the impact was probably yet to affect Wychwood. The Roman period is equally as blurred with many traditions of the Iron Age communities continuing for centuries and the influence of Roman ways of life being identifiable for decades after any political severance with Rome.

The Forest of Wychwood is a medieval concept and, as far as we can tell, did not exist in the Iron Age and Roman period. Archaeologists have made suggestions about the amount of woodland cover there was in the area at that time, but without extensive evidence these estimates remain highly speculative. Any continuous cover of primeval forest was likely to have disappeared by the Middle Iron Age when the countryside was being turned into a farmed landscape. The density of occupation in Roman times in the valleys of the Evenlode and Glyme, and the finding of Roman sites within and at the edges of the present Wychwood Forest, indicates that woodland cover might have been much less than at present.

Choosing the bounds of 'Wychwood' in the Iron Age and Roman period is inevitably an arbitrary process. Identifying the area as that encompassed by the medieval bounds of the forest would have the implication of including the archaeology of a large part of Oxfordshire and require a much more extensive and less focused book than this. So the area of 'Wychwood' will be defined as the limestone plateau; to the south the northern slopes of the valley of the River Windrush; to the west the limits of Wychwood will be the Cotswolds proper, roughly a line drawn from Burford to Chastleton; and to the north the area bounded by a line drawn through Chipping Norton, Great Tew, Middle Barton and the River Dorn to the Glyme, Evenlode and Thames Valley. In terms of the West Oxfordshire Landscape Assessment (1998) the area encompasses (from south to north) the Upper Windrush Valley, parts of Eynsham Vale, the Wychwood Uplands, the Upper Evenlode Valley, the Eastern Parks and Valleys and the Enstone Uplands. These boundaries will be slightly permeable and when a significant site occurs just outside them it will be discussed to throw further light on what happened within the area.

This defined region will have many advantages. It will allow an examination of the gradual development of a mainly rural area during the period 800 BC to AD 500 during which expanding agriculture created a fully utilised landscape. The area was an important central place in the Late Iron Age and Early Roman period through the existence of the Grim's Ditch. It contains evidence for the very early military aspects of the Roman conquest and a major Roman road, Akeman Street. Finally, it is the location of some of the earliest villas in Roman Britain, the most sumptuous villas of the later period and has one of the greatest densities of villas in Britannia. There will, of course, be disadvantages to selecting a block of land and removing it from the wider landscape. Some of these can be overcome by making reference to what was happening in the Thames Valley to the south, or the Cotswolds to the west, as these areas would certainly have influenced the activities taking place within Wychwood. What is harder to compensate for is the extremely patchy nature of the discovered archaeology within the area. This is contingent not just on a lack of inhabitation during the past, but also, and probably more significantly, by the attention given, or not as the case may be, to particular locations by archaeologists. A glance at a map of Iron Age and Roman Wychwood is more likely to give an account of archaeologists' activities than the actual number of sites that were in the area. Again, to give a balanced picture it will be necessary to invoke the research results from similar sites outside the area.

The physical environment

The defined region is cut by the valleys of the Windrush, Evenlode and Glyme which have a generally south-east trend to the Thames of which they are tributaries. At the north-west extremity of the area the land reaches 700 ft (213m) near Chipping Norton, and on the south-east boundary in the Thames Valley it drops to about 60m (200 ft).

The land use and settlement reflect soil changes, themselves dependent on the underlying geology. The rock strata dip to the south-east, but at a greater angle than the general slope of the land, and so produce these soil variations. The Oolitic limestones form the higher, plateau features of the area and being permeable have few streams or other sources of surface water. Since medieval times they have been used

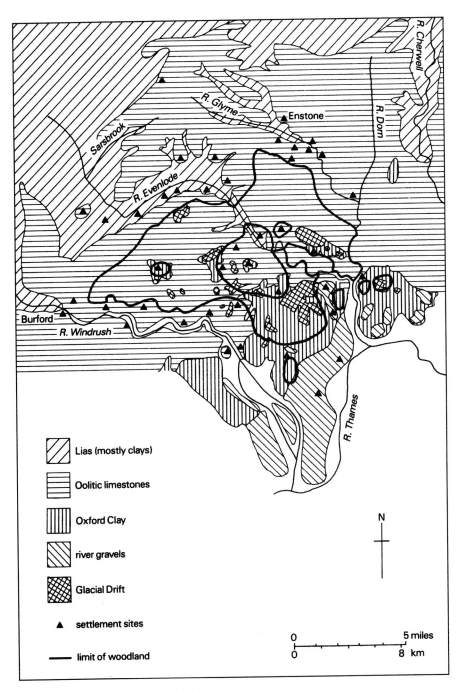

1.1 The geology of the Wychwood Region

for arable cultivation and sheep, the loamy soils being easy to cultivate. The Oolitic strata, Chipping Norton Limestone, Great Oolite and Forest Marble have been used as building stone throughout the area and further afield, though the Cornbrash, a flaggy limestone also part of the series, is unsuitable for building. Below the Oolitic series are the Liassic rocks, mostly clays, which outcrop in the Evenlode valley above Fawler and produce heavy soils which in the past were mainly grasslands, but are increasingly cultivated with modern plough technology. In the Evenlode Valley the junction of the impermeable Lias and the limestone is marked by a spring line that has attracted settlement throughout the past. Overlying the limestones in the south-eastern part of the area are the Oxford clays, with patches of Glacial Drift, both of which produce soils which are heavy and so have been used as pasture or woodland. Few streams cross the clays and water sources were generally ponds and wells.

Distinctive landscapes, reflecting the underlying geology, are found when crossing the area from east to west or north to south. Perhaps the best way of appreciating these varied locations is to visit, preferably on foot, some of the sites mentioned in the book and so gain a sense of these places.

Overview

Peopling this varied landscape in the distant past is not an easy task. Archaeology might tell us a great deal about where settlements were and what economic activities took place in them, but we have no idea of the personal response of the people to the countryside that lay around them and which they were changing daily. Nor are we able to understand how wide their horizons were, how far they could, or wished, to travel in an area which we can cross by car in half an hour. Inevitably, a book about the late prehistoric and Roman periods in a rural area will be academic and try to be objective, but sites are much more than their physical or human features and elicit an individual 'sense of place' in each of us. It is worth reflecting on this when we examine the remnants of vibrant lives that we can have no access to across the thousands of years since they existed. We find sites which we define as Iron Age or Roman and, if we are fortunate, locate evidence that gives us a range of a hundred years in which changes to the structures took place. Within that hundred years, at any settled location, several generations will have grown up and lived their lives with days or seasons as their main chronologies.

Many of us are probably interested in the past because we wish to get insights into the way people dealt with being human in less secure times. Unfortunately, because this book is not a novel or a history, this is something that we can only construct in our twenty-first century minds as we visit the sites and respond to the countryside around. However, we can be sure that the landscape we see bears the marks of our distant forebears – it would have been a different countryside without them. An even more exciting thought is that, statistically, many of them would have been our own ancestors.

2

The Sources of Evidence

Any valid account of the distant past has to be based on either documentary or archaeological evidence or both. As far as we are aware, Iron Age communities did not use the written word, so Britain enters the light of history in 55 BC and ceases to be 'prehistoric' with Julius Caesar's description of his forays into southern England. Throughout the Roman period there is sporadic documentation about the province of Britannia from which we can glean some scraps of information about political life, but there is no mention of the landscape or economy of Wychwood. While there are occasional references to the Dobunni or Catuvellauni, Iron Age tribes whose borders were in the Wychwood area, no important personages are mentioned by name. For the Iron Age and Roman periods we are completely dependent on archaeological evidence, material sources such as the remains of structures, objects and biological traces. Everything we infer about that distant time in Wychwood's past comes from the practice of archaeology. The period which is being described and analysed lasted at least a thousand years, with all the interactions of everyday life that that implies, yet the amount of archaeological evidence that we are aware of is very limited considering the timescale.

Archaeological materials vary in their nature and importance in both the Iron Age and the Roman period. The basic evidence consists of sites, with their associated landscape features, and objects. While Roman written sources were often intended to ensure the future was aware of the actions of a particular people in the past, much of the archaeological evidence exists because of accidental loss and survival. As such, archaeological evidence tends to represent all classes of people rather than just an elite, and gives us an opportunity to get a broader picture of everyday life.

Structures: buildings and settlements

The type of sites that characterise the Iron Age and Roman periods in Wychwood are very different, though many landscape features such as field shapes probably stayed constant. During the Iron Age it would appear that timber

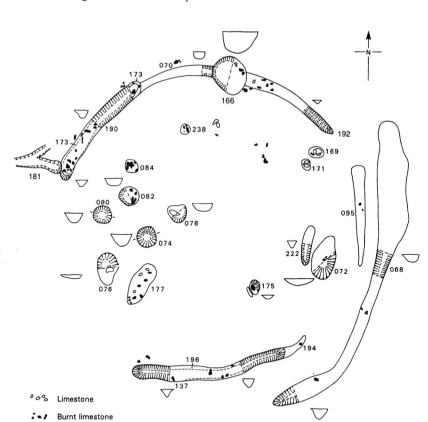

2.1 The post holes, pits and ditches of the round-house at the middle Iron Age settlement at Deer Park Road, Witney. (OAHS: *Oxoniensia* 60,76)

was the main structural material in the majority of dwellings and the favoured method of demarcating settlements or tracts of land was with banks, hedges and ditches. The wood that was used in the construction of round-houses and industrial or farm buildings has not survived, leaving cavities that contain the rotted material or have later been filled in with soil. Similarly, the ditches that surrounded occupation sites have also been gradually filled in by weathering degrading their accompanying banks or were deliberately back-filled by subsequent occupation. These factors cause problems for the discovery of sites and consequently we are able to identify very few Iron Age settlements within the Wychwood area. The most recognisable Iron Age sites today are the results of massive earthmoving projects such as hill forts or the North Oxfordshire Grim's Ditch whose remains still form significant features in the landscape. It is interesting that the only traces we have of Iron Age buildings in the central area of Wychwood are those found below Grim's Ditch or the Roman villas where excavations have taken place, and these only amount to a few post holes with no coherent plan.

During the Roman period early military structures were also composed of timber and turf or soil with similar problems for identification, though with important exceptions which will be examined later. However, as the area became more Romanised many settlements, villas and small towns were constructed in more durable materials. Structures were made of different materials: wood, stone, brick and tile each of which has different rates of survival both when upstanding and when buried. The type of material being used greatly influences present-day chances of identifying sites where human beings dwelt or stored materials. The plans of many Roman structures still survive below the ground as the foundation courses of walls. However, good building stone is always at a premium even where it can be had locally by quarrying. Over the centuries the stone that was used in the Roman villas will have been reused many times, some perhaps only robbed out of the original site in recent centuries. However, many low-status dwellings in Wychwood during the Roman period continued to use timber in their construction and are almost completely unidentifiable. We are much more aware of specific elements of the Roman landscape because the stone of the villas and farms, as well as the roadside settlements, are much easier to locate that the filled-in post-holes of timber structures.

Upstanding structures from both the Iron Age and the Roman periods are rare in Wychwood. The banks of the Iron Age hillforts that have survived do so because they crest land too steep to plough and which has been given over to woodland for much of the past. The steepness of the relief that was responsible for the original choice of a defendable site has also been the major factor in their survival. Some elements of the Grim's Ditch survive above ground but only where they have been protected by woodland over many centuries or where they have remained useful markers of territory. Even then it is sometimes difficult to be certain that these discontinuous stretches of bank were connected to others. Within the woodland of Wychwood Forest and Ditchley there are no doubt remnants of banks that formed the boundaries of settlement or were used for herding animals into specific areas, but the density of woodland makes it difficult to identify or make sense of them. In areas used as parkland for long periods and not subjected to ploughing upstanding remains can be seen also. In Blenheim Park are the notable remains of a stretch of Grim's Ditch and the slight earthworks of a religious site, which are now covered by a conifer plantation. In Cornbury the ditch and ramparts of two Roman rectangular marching camps still stand proud above the short grassland of the deer park.

Centuries of ploughing have flattened earthworks, even banks that were over

2.2 Upstanding remains of the North Oxfordshire Grim's Ditch in Blenheim Park unaffected by ploughing. (Author)

a metre high like that which formed the North Oxfordshire Grim's Ditch. They have been smoothed away or deliberately slighted by agricultural processes.

Quarrying and building by subsequent generations also make the retrieval of a complete picture of the landscape impossible.

Objects

Objects were designed with a purpose and by identifying that purpose we can try to reconstruct some of the everyday activities that helped people survive. However, objects also suffer the same problem of decay depending on what they were made of and their histories after they were discarded or lost. Fragmentary ceramic vessels, building debris, food refuse, especially animal bones and infrequent metal objects such as coins, personal ornaments and household equipment provide archaeologists with information about past lifestyles and economies. Not all materials survive the passage of time. Usually objects made of biological materials such as wood, leather and cloth are unlikely to survive and this limits the information that can be recovered. Presumably, wooden objects and leather articles were used for a great many activities on both Iron Age and Roman sites, but the chances of locating them in our area are slim as they would only survive over long periods in waterlogged conditions which stop the action of oxygen leading to decay. Such anaerobic conditions are rare in a limestone landscape. However, the limestone derived soils of the Wychwood area are not acidic and this aids the survival of bones and pottery, perhaps the most frequent finds on sites.

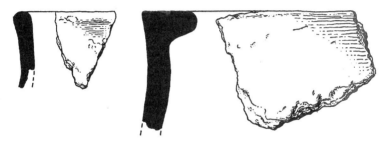

2.3 Early Iron Age pottery from Lyneham Camp, (OAHS: *Oxoniensia* 22, 6)

The most common material found on archaeological sites is pottery. The clay and its tempering materials can been turned into a stone and glass-like consistency through firing at high temperatures, and this enables it to survive for long periods. However, if the clay is not fired completely or has been formed from course materials leaving voids in the clay, survival into the present is not good, and a fragment of pottery ploughed to the surface will collapse under the stresses of the expansion of water in its voids during frosty periods leaving an unrecognisable collection of grains. This is frequently the case with Iron Age pottery, which was produced by a 'cottage' industry in the local rural area, and results in difficulties in identifying ceramic materials of the period in the field.

In the Roman period potting becomes more sophisticated and technology allowed higher kiln temperatures to be maintained for longer periods. Pots were traded over large distances with the better made products gaining ready markets. The variety of sources for local pots are as wide as France for sophisticated, red-glazed Samian ware to Dorset for very course Black Burnished Ware, but mainly we find the products of the large Oxford industries. Pottery is invaluable in aiding the recognition of Roman sites, especially those with no building materials. It also enables us to broadly date sites with reference to pottery found elsewhere that has been dated from coins found in the same context.

Clay was also used in the manufacture of tile, both for roofs and as ducts for the hot fumes of hypocausts. Many of the tile fragments contain chalk inclusions indicating a kiln source near Minety in Wiltshire.

Glass has an excellent survival rate, for the same reasons as pottery – its manufacturing processes. Being expensive to produce it was often used in exquisite domestic vessels, and less rarely as window glass, giving an indicator of the status of the owner of a villa.

Occasionally monumental stone carvings of a religious nature are found, but this has been a rare occurrence in Wychwood except in the villas. Architectural fragments of carved stone enable us to see the 'Roman' elements in the design of these country houses. However many examples were made from local or imported limestone and may have been burnt in later times to produce lime to spread on the

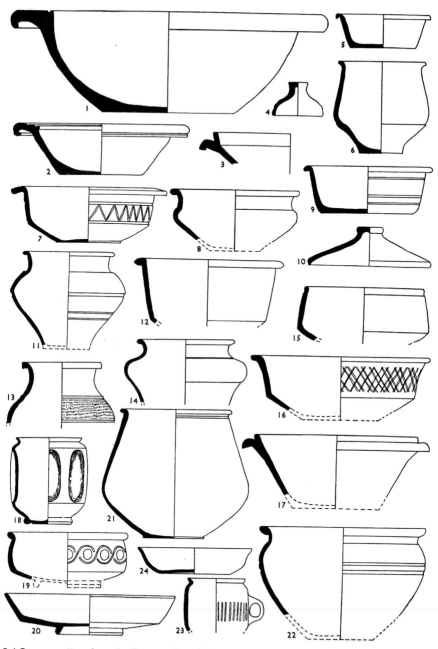

2.4 Coarse pottery from the Roman villa at Ditchley. (OAHS: *Oxoniensia* 1, 58)

fields. Very few inscriptions have been found, with the exceptions of the names SATAVACUS and BELLICIA incised on a set of clay pipes (see page viii) and ANNA and SENTICA scratched onto pots at Shakenoak, and there are no examples of tombstones, so individual people of the period are 'invisible' to us.

Stone and clay were used in the creation of the mosaic pavements found at North Leigh and Stonesfield villas and suspected elsewhere from the retrieval of individual tesserae. These pavements were very labour-intensive to produce and clearly belonged to well-to-do owners. They give us an insight into trading patterns as many were made by Cirencester craftsmen and sometimes are indicators of the degree of Romanisation of a person through the inclusion of images of deities such as Bacchus at Stonesfield. Stone was also used in the Roman period for roofing (Iron Age huts were probably roofed with straw or turf) and some of this material originates in the Stonesfield area which had a significant 'slate' industry in the medieval period.

Coins are valuable indicators of the dates of sites but they also give us an insight into the political climate of the time of their production through the iconography and inscriptions on their obverse and reverse. Iron Age coins have been recovered occasionally as chance finds, but since coinage was not used in the modern way, we would not expect to recover large numbers of them. However, they can help us to identify contemporary tribal territories though as yet a large enough, valid sample has yet to be accumulated in Wychwood. Only five silver coins have been found in the area, some of them now untraceable, but they give us the names of rulers of the Dobunni: CURIO, BODVOC, COMUX, EISV. Roman coins have been found more frequently, mainly on excavations, and are valuable for dating the sites through the image and legend of individual emperors, though as the fifth century is reached, coinage becomes rarer in the country as a whole.

Other metal objects, particularly those made of bronze and iron, survive well in the limestone soils. The list of metal finds from Shakenoak Roman villa gives us a wide view of many aspects of everyday life from agricultural tools to furni-

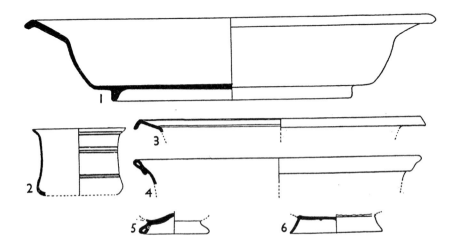

2.5 Glass vessels from the Roman villa at Ditchley. (OAHS: *Oxoniensia* 1,63)

2.6 Bronze terret from the Roman villa at Ditchley. (OAHS: *Oxoniensia* 1,55)

ture fittings to personal ornaments. This latter enable us to get close to the personal tastes of individuals in a way that no other common find can.

Animal bones are good indicators of diet on a site, and from them we are able to see changes of diet from the Iron Age, where pig dominates, to the Roman period with its emphasis on cattle. However, bones do not necessarily give a good indication of the farming regime as many of the animals might have been taken elsewhere, on the hoof, for slaughter. Animal bone was also used for a variety of objects in the Roman period such as pins, needles and combs.

The analysis of soils, timber fragments (particularly as charcoal which survives more frequently), snail shells and pollen (which is almost indestructible) has enabled biologists to suggest what the landscape looked like in the past. Samples of biological materials from the villas at Callow Hill and Shakenoak have given us a 'window' into the vegetation surrounding the settlements and this was also achieved for the Iron Age site at Deer Park in Witney.

Archaeological techniques

Archaeologists have developed methods for identifying buried sites of this period. The best known, but least used, is excavation in which a site is systematically exposed and the sequence and nature of the occupation is seen in the plans of the structures and layers of the soil that indicate how the buried deposits accumulated. The objects found enable archaeologists to relate activities on a particular site to those happening elsewhere at the time. In Wychwood there have been a small number of excavations in the past, mainly on the more easily identifiable high-status villas. These excavations, many of which were undertaken before the

Second World War, have given us some insights into the shapes and chronological development of the structures and the type of activities that took place.

Getting a wide view of the landscape has been made easier by the development of aerial photography. The identification of soil marks has enabled buried features such as ditches and banks to be recognised from the air. This technique can be successful due to the differential colouring of soils, with filled ditches often being darker than that of the surrounding landscape and the stony nature of a degraded bank being lighter. However, due to the stone of the built structures in Wychwood being from the parent rock, limestone, they are very difficult to identify. Crop marks are also valuable indicators of buried sites. When a suitable crop, such as wheat, comes under stress during periods of drought, plants over buried ditches are able to access deeper supplies of moisture and are likely to be of a darker colour than those over buried walls which cannot capture the water needed and are less well developed and lighter. Through these processes the walls of buried structures, ditches and wells can be identified and the famous aerial photographs of Ditchley villa taken in the 1930s were a confirmation of the effectiveness of the technique of aerial photography. However, the flimsy structures of the Iron Age are unlikely to be discovered by this method though the ditches around enclosures do show up under the right conditions.

Wychwood has been the focus of many archaeological and commercial flights to record the landscape from the air and there is a large collection of aerial photos taken from the 1930s onwards recording not only buried features, but the rapidly changing shape of the landscape. Perhaps one of the most important factors in our exploration of the past landscape was the siting of airfields in the area during the Second World War, particularly the American base at Upper Heyford. Sorties flown over the area designed to train reconnaissance photographers have left us with a rich legacy of historic photos of a vanished landscape. These images are collected at the Royal Commission for Historic Monuments in Swindon and show us a landscape much changed since the 1940s. Most obviously we see a much more wooded land with smaller fields and often farm buildings that have disappeared. Aerial photography can increase our knowledge of the surviving evidence substantially and coupled with a suitable summer our ideas of the shape and use of the landscape can change significantly. However, the opportunities for the recovery of archaeological information within Wychwood are not as good as in places such as the flood plains of river valleys which are much more susceptible to crop mark formation on alluvium.

Another technique, which is very labour intensive, is fieldwalking. When buried sites are ploughed building materials and objects are disturbed and deposited on the surface of a field. In the past the ploughman walked close to the ground behind his team and it was possible to recognise building materials and

2.7 An aerial view of the Roman villa at Ditchley (Ashmolean Museum)

objects as they were turned up by plough or disinterred from clods of earth by the harrow. Many of the Roman sites were discovered in this manner, for example Ditchley which was known about at least as early as 1857. Now the mechanisation of agriculture has robbed us of this intimate view of the surface of the land. Today ploughing is undertaken from large machines with the driver perched high above the soil and the chance finds of the past do not occur. Nowadays it is systematic walking and collection of the materials on a gridded area that can reveal the location of sites and the approximate date of the underlying structures can be inferred from the finds. Obviously sites that are ploughed regularly are more likely to be found than those under woodland or permanent pasture. However, it is difficult to infer the status of a structure from surface finds only. Most fields in the Wychwood landscape will provide a 'background noise' of Roman pottery since many of the broken pots ended up on the manure heap and their fragments would have been widely scattered across the arable landscape. Sometimes intense scatters of pottery can be identified during fieldwalking which may indicate a Roman period site. If those scatters also have roof tile then we can presume that there was a structure close by as roof tile is not something that gets carried far from a decayed or demolished building. If fragments of combed hypocaust tile are found, there is even more likelihood that the site below was of high status as this sort of material is unlikely to be reused and more likely to be left in situ after the demise of a structure; indeed, because it is so embedded in the fabric of a structure's walls, it is almost certain to have been moved only by subsequent ploughing. In attempting to locate villa structures in the Ditchley area, which has an intense distribution of these types of dwelling, the presence of hypocaust tile can be used as the main indicator of status. Little systematic field-walking has taken place in the Wychwood area, though the work of groups and individuals around the Wychwoods, Charlbury and Ditchley shows the effectiveness of the technique. They have revealed sites otherwise unidentifiable on the ground or from the air and of especial importance have been several sites producing Roman pottery but not building materials. These indicate the locations of low status, non-villa settlements that were probably very common and well distributed throughout the landscape.

Within the area there has been limited use of non-invasive geophysical techniques that can explore the structures below the soil without destroying them. This is a cheaper and more site-friendly method than excavation and in the future it is possible that many more explorations of this nature will take place.

Today, the most likely method of finding new sites on the ground, and there are probably still the majority to be found, is by a targeted strategy using air photos, fieldwalking or excavation in advance of development. Unfortunately, there is not much activity of this sort taking place with the inevitable results for the finding of new sites.

Archaeologists' own interests can also skew the overall picture. The majority of excavations in the Wychwood area have been undertaken on Roman villas. These are more likely to produce structures of quality and the sites are more easily found. Fewer archaeologists have been interested in the Iron Age remains, though projects have been carried out on the North Oxfordshire Grim's Ditch which is more visible in the landscape. The distribution of known sites is likely to be a function of the distribution of professional or amateur archaeologists and their interests.

The interpretation of this archaeological material will depend on the personalities who are constructing the past of Wychwood and the period in which they are doing it. The amount of knowledge available and the interest and experience of the archaeologist will be crucial factors in the creation of a picture of the past in a particular place and it is only by examining archaeological work in the context of its time that we can see how evidence for Wychwood's past has been recovered and how that past has been constructed.

3

The Discovery of Iron Age and Roman Wychwood

The past has happened and doesn't exist any more. While there might be a large amount of evidence available for Iron Age and Roman periods in the Wychwood area it cannot produce an account by itself – it is dumb. The surviving evidence needs to be identified and interpreted by human beings who then make a mental construction of what might have happened at a particular time in a particular place. The mental constructions that people make depend on their previous experience of the type of evidence, so the more a person knows about a particular period the more valid that construction might be. However, the life experience of an individual and the values they hold will also colour their attempts at constructions of the past. This means that there have been many 'pasts' of Iron Age and Roman Wychwood which have evolved through increasing acquaintance with a growing body of evidence and the various values held by society and individuals at the time the constructions were made.

We know little about what people thought about the distant past of Wychwood before the early 18th century. Books such as William Camden's *Britannia*, first published in Latin in 1586, give general descriptions of an anti-quarian character of a few sites, and Dr. Robert Plot's *The Natural History of Oxfordshire* (1677) also refers to some archaeological remains in Wychwood in passing, but it is mainly concerned with natural resources and phenomena. However, it is hard to imagine that chance finds by ploughmen who worked so close to the soil they turned, or in the digging of foundations for houses, did not cause speculation among the local people.

From the early 18th century to the present there have been a growing number of systematic efforts to locate evidence for the Iron Age and Roman periods and to use it to construct the life styles of the previous inhabitants. Inevitably, there has been an accumulation of knowledge that has changed our views of life in the area at that time and also a change in attitudes to the past. This 'discovery' of Iron Age and Roman Wychwood is best explored through a series of case studies from the early 18th to the late 20th centuries and throughout the Wychwood area that demonstrate how techniques for retrieving evidence have developed, the growth of understanding has occurred, and attitudes to the past have changed.

1712: Hearne and the Stonesfield Villa

The discovery of the Stonesfield mosaic was controversial. Even the date of the unearthing of the pavement is subject to some contention. In the version of the tenant farmer, a local man named Handes, the coloured and elaborately designed mosaic pavement, thirty-five feet long and twenty feet wide was found on Friday 25th January 1712 at Chesthill Acre Farm, or Chestrenhill (the 'chester' element of the name often indicates Roman remains somewhere close by), near Stonesfield. He insisted that he was ploughing a field when he discovered some large stones in the soil. When he lifted them to inspect the ground underneath, he discovered an ancient 'urn' and what appeared to be a tiled pavement. However, later enquiries suggested that Handes had found the mosaic several weeks earlier but kept the discovery to himself until he could re-negotiate the lease with the stipulation that he could 'dig the ground', and only then did he 'discover' the pavement.

One of the first of the many antiquaries to visit the site of the discovery was Thomas Hearne. Hearne was an antiquary, a collector of objects and a visitor to ancient sites, resident at St. Edmund Hall in Oxford. As Underkeeper at the Bodleian Library he was in the perfect position to follow his two great interests, the histories of Rome and England, which the Stonesfield pavement brought together. At first he was very sceptical about the description of the design on the pavement which was reported as featuring Apollo riding a serpent or dragon with pheasants and flower pots. He though rather the figure was St. Michael killing the dragon with 'his spear in his left hand' and identified the shoes of the figure as being medieval. He considered the pavement as originating from a manor house of some local dignitary rather than being Roman. His scepticism was increased when he was told that the urn had disintegrated and was nowhere to be seen. When a horde of Roman coins that had been said to have been discovered near the pavement appeared to be a small amount of local finds planted to attract visitors, his doubts were reinforced. However, being a meticulous recorder, he entered into his notebook that the pavement had been covered with rubbish, pieces of stones and slate, great broad bricks, coal and corn.

News about the pavement spread rapidly and distantly and gave rise to much speculation. On 14th February the Secretary of the Royal Society announced the find to a meeting in London. During the discussion afterwards it was suggested that the pavement was from a Roman general's tent – a 'praetorium'. This indicates the overwhelmingly military conception of the Roman occupation of Britain prevalent at the time. Several Oxford men visited the site and drew the design which was then generally believed to be of Bacchus with a tiger. At the end of February a large group of scholars from Oxford came to Stonesfield led by Edmund Halley, the astronomer and Professor of Geometry. It was typical of the times that intellectuals were interested in learned discussion of every kind. Halley had news of the pavement on 20th February: 'It is indeed a Site worth seeing the Mosaick work intire and the colours as fresh as I believe at the first laying', his informant wrote. However, the image on the mosaic was described as 'a Briton with a spear doubly barb'd mounted upon a dragon with a long taile and webb'd feet.' Halley didn't see the alleged find of coins either and found the antiquaries in his party arguing whether the pavement was Roman or Saxon. At this time so few examples of mosaics had been found that it was not obvious, as it might be to even the casual observer today, that such features were indicative of the Roman period. Halley also thought the figure was a Bacchus and the animal a tiger and noticed that the wheat found there was 'very soft and friable'. Another visitor, Tilleman Bobart, a botanist, described the scene at Stonesfield:

> There are many spectators daily to see it, and very different in their opinions of its former use. Some suppose it to have been a Roman temple, others a Generall's tent, and some a place to burn their dead bodies, their having been found remains of humane bones and burnt wheat.

Meanwhile Handes was charging five pounds for drawing the mosaic in the field and this led to a number of secret sketches by visitors or drawings from memory away from the site, which further compounded the confusion.

Hearne was eventually convinced by those who had access to the growing antiquarian literature of the time: 'Upon more mature Consideration', he wrote 'I am persuaded t'was a Roman Praetorium, and can answer all Objections'. He was prepared to walk the distance from Oxford to Stonesfield and he visited the pavement at least eight times. On each visit he made copious notes. He identified the design as portraying Apollo, and indicated that the pavement was of the later Roman period, perhaps from a general's villa. He even suggested a date for the making of the mosaic: the year AD 369 when the Emperor Theodosius visited Britain. As late as April 21 he noted: 'A great many People go still to see this Curiosity' (a popular word among antiquaries). Hearne published his opinions in 'Discourse Concerning the Stonesfield Pavement' with an accompanying drawing as part of a larger book, his *Itinerary*. This showed considerable insight in identifying the function of the pavement as being in the dining room of a 'rich Gentlemen'. He also correctly identified the hypocaust flues visible at the side of

Scale [scale bar] 0 1 2 3 4 5 Feet

3.1 Mosaic pavement from Stonesfield engraved by William Lewington (*Victoria County History*).

the pavement as being for heating rather than water. The publication won over a number of followers to the Apollo theory but not all.

John Pointer, a collector of 'curiosities' and a chaplain to Merton College objected to the Apollo designation. In his publication on the Stonesfield pavement, he quoted a number of learned accounts of how Bacchus was represented in Roman mythology. He also thought that the pavement was 'the most elaborate Piece of Roman Workmanship of this sort and One of the Finest in all Britain'. Unfortunately for Hearne, Pointer's identification was supported by many of his contemporaries. Hearne may have thought that Pointer's work was a 'silly, illiterate, mean account' but he lost the day.

The end of the story of the Stonesfield pavement is equally as bizarre as its discovery. In the autumn of 1712 Hearne again visited the mosaic which was by then much damaged and he feared for it during the frosts and rains of winter. Handes had made his money from the attraction, and had numerous rows with the owner of the land as to how the profits should be split. Clearly both had lost interest in the feature and neither had the wherewithal to protect it permanently and did not consider burying it for protection. The result was that fragments of the mosaic were pilfered and taken to the surrounding villages, there to disappear or crumble.

The whole affair has the feel of a circus with large numbers of people visiting the site, Handes no doubt making money from his attraction, as well as other local people cashing in by selling food and drink and perhaps other ancient objects found in the fields that surround Stonesfield. Though, eventually, the age of the pavement and the iconography of the design were recognised, the varied conjectures show us something about the state of knowledge of the past, its value and the problems of dating discoveries.

Further excavations were to take place in 1779–80 when the mosaic was again found in a tolerable state of preservation. Other excavations located a well, a bath and a cistern close by. The excavations were possibly under the patronage of the Duke of Marlborough, who had also been excavating Akeman Street where it enters Blenheim Park. This time everything was measured and drawn precisely making it possible to see the Stonesfield mosaic within the perspective of a larger structure. Thomas Warton, the Rector of Kiddington, had the foresight to suggest that the villa may have been built by a wealthy Celtic family who must have eventually built in Roman style. Antiquarianism was slowly metamorphosing into archaeology.

The pavement was opened again in 1802 by William Fowler to make a new engraving and found to be in good preservation. Ten years later it was thought that local people had again destroyed all of the pavements and an excavation to locate them was abandoned and attention turned to the North Leigh Villa which was being excavated at this time.

Today nothing is visible on the site and the exact location of the Stonesfield pavement has been lost. It would be easy to be dismissive of the local people who took parts of the pavement for keep-sakes, but as recently as the 1990s two mosaics, one at Worsham and the other at Widford, have had to be covered over to stop the depredations of souvenir hunters.

1813-16: Hakewill and North Leigh

The Rector of Kiddington, Thomas Warton, identified the ruins of North Leigh villa and mentioned them in his *History of Kiddington* in 1783.

> In the romantic valley between Stunsfield and Northleigh, and not half a mile from the Akeman-street, are the vestiges of a Roman OFFICINA, or laboratory, never mentioned by any writer, for making bricks, tiles and stucco. The area was lately a spreading tumulus, consisting of rubbish and fragments of Roman bricks and cement, and probably concealing ovens, hypocaustic ducts, and subterraneous works of stone, necessary for that manufacture, in which the Romans excelled.

Even in the light of the Stonesfield find, the idea of a 'villa' was not yet current and the remains at North Leigh were seen as a workshop complex. The field had been known as 'Roman Piece' and in 1813 the villa remains were showing as a rectangular earthwork and were rediscovered by a local clergyman who found bricks and tiles after ploughing.

Henry Hakewill (1771-1830), who excavated the site in the years 1813-16, was an architect who among other things was responsible for the re-building of Rugby School, work at Blenheim Palace, Cornbury Park and alterations to the Radcliffe Camera and Infirmary. The report on his work at North Leigh was published as 'An Account of the Roman Villa discovered at Northleigh, Oxfordshire, in the years 1813-14-15-16' in Skelton's *Antiquities of Oxfordshire*, 1823, and re-issued separately in 1826. It begins by setting the site into context with a map showing the known Roman remains: Callow Hill, Ditchley, Bury Close, Stonesfield and North Leigh. With the exception of Fawler (discovered when the Oxford-Worcester railway was built in 1853) and Shakenoak villas and the Lee's Rest shrine, the list contains all the important sites known today. The excavations began in the autumn of 1813 and lasted for four seasons.

The first season produced walls around a quadrangle and many tesserae. 'It was concluded that the building was of Roman origin and that some of the rooms in it had been decorated with tessellated pavements'. Such a confident statement indicates the growth in knowledge since the discovery of the Stonesfield pavement a hundred years previously.

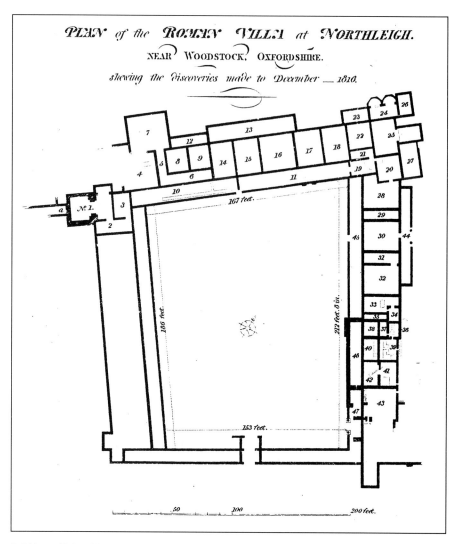

3.2 Henry Hakewill's 1816 plan of North Leigh Roman villa (*Victoria County History*).

Over the next four years, with the exception of 1814 when the field was under tillage, the site was explored gradually. The excavation began with the northern side and continued in 1816 on the western side.

From time to time the remains of a hypocaust, a very curious bath, several rooms with coarse tessellated floors, and a small one with a pavement of much finer materials, were found and in the month of October (1815) the investigation was rewarded by the discovery of the large room containing a very beautiful Mosaic pavement, 28 feet (8.5 m) long by 22 feet (6.7 m) wide.

The mosaic is still on view at the site. A further series of baths were discovered in 1816,

> but the unusual state of the weather made it impossible to superintend the search, and it was thought better to employ the men (where less care was necessary) in tracing the exterior walls of the building, and particularly these which connected the north and south sides.

Neither the north or south sides were excavated completely, but the sensitivity of the exploration techniques is clear and a direct contrast to the Stonesfield debacle.

Hakewill sought to explain the formation of the site and included an illustrated section of the soil beneath part of a broken pavement (perhaps one of the earliest section drawings in British archaeology).

> On examining the substratum … where the pavement was broken, it was ascertained that it was supported by stones placed edgeways on the ground; and that to the depth of eight feet the natural soil and rock had been removed, and the cavity filled with rubbish. Many oyster-shells and pieces of broken pottery were found at the bottom of this cavity.

Hakewill didn't consider that these layers might have accumulated through the previous occupation of this part of the site and that they could give indications of its previous development. The concept of interpreting a stratigraphic section in this way was not to be formalised in archaeology until the work of Pitt-Rivers in the 1870s. At North Leigh it was to take until 1910 before excavation explored the implications of this section in terms of earlier structures. However, Hakewill did consider the

3.3 Hakewill's section drawing at North Leigh

post-villa occupation of the structure when describing the rough dry stone walls which had been built over the floors and signs of burning on the mosaics; he noted that 'the building had in later times afforded shelter to a very humble class of inhabitants, by whom convenience only was consulted, without any regard to the refinements of taste, or reverence for ancient grandeur'. Such lack of respect still prevailed in the area at the time of the excavation for, on the discovery of a mosaic, 'such was the curiosity of the local country people, who, on the Sunday following the discovery, flocked in crowds to the spot, that before any precautions could be adopted the pavement was much injured'.

Hakewill was much taken with the site. 'The situation of this villa is well chosen; for the little valley in which it is placed, and the scenery around it, are remarkably beautiful'. He follows this statement with a detailed account of the view in every direction. What is more remarkable about his report is the detailed description of the ground plan room by room. Measurements are given and the detail of the evidence carefully described before any interpretation is given. He suggests how the hypocaust system works with some flues discharging smoke while others carried heat under the floors, details changes made over time by recognising contrasting wall sizes and directions and makes comparisons with buildings described in Roman literature. Clearly, Hakewill expected others to work on the villa remains in the future and he is careful to list those rooms which were not excavated or 'imperfectly examined'.

Hakewill's report has much detail and is especially valuable for the scaled map. However, as an architect, he is concerned only for the structure and with the exception of some identified coins and a spoon 'of white metal... very sound and perfect' there is hardly any mention of finds such as pottery or bone. The meticulous recording of the structure is not matched by detailed positioning and description of finds as the dating possibilities of pottery or its ability to suggest the function of areas of the villa was not yet realised. However, his report does give a very definite sense of place, and the preoccupation with the 'picturesque' of the time in which it was written. It was to be at least a hundred years before another excavation of equal quality was to take place in the Wychwood area.

1881: Brabrook, Price and White at Chastleton Camp

We are not aware of any excavations in Wychwood during the period 1820–80, although it is likely that there was some antiquarian work which was not reported formally. Perhaps the most significant archaeological event was the visit of General Lane Fox (later to become the influential archaeologist Pitt-Rivers) to Ditchley, which was the home of his wife's uncle, Lord Dillon, in April 1868. It likely from the detail of his knowledge that he had paid many visits to

Ditchley and got to know the area well. In a paper published in the same year he identifies the sites of Roman villas, one of which is 'missing' today, and comments on Grim's Ditch, identifying its unbroken course from Callow Hill to Cornbury. He reported that while walking the field in which the Callow Hill villa was situated he also found worked flint and made the assumption that the Romans also used flint, rather than that the site had been sequentially occupied.

Excavations took place at Chastleton Camp, or Fort or Burrow (know known to be a late Bronze Age or early Iron Age site) in, or shortly before, 1881 and were briefly reported by J. E. Price in the *Journal of the Royal Anthropological Institute of Great Britain* for 1881. The three excavators were all Fellows of the Society of Antiquaries of London and from their obituaries in its journal it is possible to define some of their interests and backgrounds. Edward William Brabrook, knighted in 1904, was for his working life Assistant Registrar and Registrar of Friendly Societies. He had wide interests and became President of the Royal Anthropological Institute, the Folk Lore Society and the South Eastern Union of Scientific Societies among others and was a member of the Royal Statistical Society and the Royal Society for Literature. John E. Price was a 'City' man but also a 'devoted Antiquary' and a principal authority on the Roman occupation of London. Among his major achievements were the publication of the excavation of the Roman villa at Brading on the Isle of Wight and a descriptive account of the Guildhall of the City of London. Arthur White also had expertise on Roman London though his 'communications' to the Society of Antiquaries included descriptions of a Roman object from Rochester and a medieval chalice. Archaeology was still a gentleman's pursuit in 1881 and access to sites for archaeological work depended on the goodwill of the gentry who owned the land. These three men were obviously well connected and sought to ensure those connections were maintained, for the report begins with an effusive acknowledgement of the landowner and others involved in the project,

> The suggestion that excavations would be of value is due to our friend and Colleague, George Harris Esq., LL.D., F.S.A. ...(who) was present on the occasion, and in readiness to receive the party who responded to the generous invitation of Miss Jones to inspect, not only the camp, but Chastleton House and the many objects of interest it contained.

Immediately one gets the sense of a social event as much as of a scientific endeavour. The classical leanings of the three excavators become apparent almost immediately with the description of the camp being a 'Castrum', a Latin term more usually applied to Roman military installations, and with the suggestion that the name Chastleton is derived from 'Cestreton' which in turn evolved from 'Castrum'.

3.4 Bone pin from Chastleton (*Victoria County History*)

The excavation strategy is impossible to ascertain: 'pits were sunk and trenches cut' but there is no indication of where these were sited as no plan was published. The ramparts do seem to have been sectioned as the structure of the bank is reported to have been of massive blocks of Oolite and 'is a monument of great labour'. There is no mention of an outer ditch, and its absence is implied by the comment that the construction is different from the usual practice of ramparts 'being formed out of earth thrown up from the outer ditch'. Finds from the ramparts included deposits of pottery, burnt bones and charcoal. Other objects included a bone pin 'of neat workmanship', a flint flake, burnt pebbles and various burnt shells.

The animal bones were examined by George Rolleston who gives a further clue to the nature of the excavations in his introduction; 'I was reluctantly obliged to decline to join the excursion to Chastleton, but I have been favoured with a small box of bones from that pleasant place'. This confirms the social and recreational aspect of the excavation which was not untypical of the time. The bones were mainly of domestic animals, pig, cow, sheep, horse, and showed indications that they had been broken by men or dogs for food, but none of humans or dogs or cats were retrieved. Three examples of water rat jaws were found to be interesting as 'they are just the parts which the polecat leaves behind'. Rolleston had found 'handfuls' of these jaws in the lairs of polecats elsewhere and presumed that this must be the case at Chastleton, even though he admits that the polecat is a river hunter and the nearest river to the camp is at least a mile away.

Rolleston could not see why the bones should be 'not nearer to us than some 500 years or so'. However Price states, 'There is nothing, therefore, in the objects found to illustrate a period, either earlier or later than the Roman occupation'. These conclusions appear to be based on tenuous links with classical sources. The finds of burnt bones and charcoal were seen as evidence that agrimensores, or Roman land surveyors, had marked the limits of the territory under Roman occupation. Price comments on a fine old ash tree on the left of one of the entrances, 'the last of four which occupied similar positions on either side of the entrances to the camp'. This he finds further compelling evidence for the work of Roman land surveyors for trees 'were often used as terminal marks, and in the selection of the four ash trees we discern a survival of this practice'. He notes that trees for such a purpose were usually brought from a distance, quoting examples of Constantinople and Carthage, and then identifies the ash as being rare in the

Chastleton district. The shape of the camp was probably the most convincing evidence. Its outlines are today somewhere between a circle and a square, but Price saw a rectangular form with rounded corners indicative of a Roman fort. The excavation 'proved that the whole of the camp is of Roman construction' and not a 'Danish barrow' as had been though previously. It was not for permanent occupation but constructed to meet some 'pressing' emergency. It would seem that the most conclusive evidence that the camp was constructed on the engineered principles was that it adjoined 'Akeman Street' and was on the borders of three counties. The imprecise nature of the report is indicated not only in it brevity and lack of detail but also in errors of fact. The Roman road at four miles distance from Chastleton Camp is Fosse Way, and one of the three counties is identified wrongly, it being Warwickshire rather than Worcestershire.

The 1881 excavation was typical in its conclusions of many other ventures of that period. Little was known of the Iron Age, classical sources had denigrated the pre-Roman occupants of the such sites as primitive, often for propaganda reasons, and excavators were steeped in classical culture in the universities. The Victorian imperialist ethic found resonances in assigning structures of the large proportions of Chastleton Camp to the Romans, 'affording further proof of Britain having been included in the same system of organisation as that which prevailed in other provinces of the Empire'.

1928-9: Leeds at Chastleton Camp

During the period between 1881 and the late 1920s we are only aware of one small excavation taking place within the Wychwood area, in Blenheim Park at the junction of Akeman Street and the Grim's Ditch in 1898. There was also a plan (since lost) made of Fawler Roman Villa by Mr Warde Fowler of Kingham who used the recollections of an old inhabitant who remembered the Great Western Railway being driven through the site. It was not until 1928–9 that large-scale activity took place and that was again at Chastleton Camp under Edward Thurlow Leeds. Leeds was successively Assistant Keeper and Keeper in the Ashmolean Museum. His character and tastes 'were those of a gentleman farmer who loved and understood the country and its background'. (Obituary, *Oxford Magazine*, Nov. 24 1935.) Brought up in the Fenlands near Peterborough, his father was interested in geology and palaeontology, and this rubbed off on the young Leeds. After university at Cambridge he entered the service of the Federated Malay States and was sent to China for two years to learn Chinese, but had to return to England as his health broke down. As an archaeologist he was single-minded and conscientious, 'he never knew what idleness was'. His obituary in the *Times* of 18 August 1955 shows this aspect of his character well; 'Genuine enquirers who asked no unwarranted favours and manifested an appropriately humble approach were received with all due kindness and attention and given every help with their work, but all who took liberties within the Museum's precincts were rebuffed in no uncertain fashion'. He laid the foundations of modern archaeological research in Oxfordshire recording minutely all he saw and producing sound interpretations.

The report of the excavation of 1928-9 at Chastleton Camp criticised fairly the techniques of the excavation fifty years earlier, and underlines the directness of his personality:

> It is hard in the light of the requirements of archaeology of our own time to imagine an account at once so unsatisfactory, with conclusions so erroneous and so unwarranted by the evidence. At the same time, in 1880 knowledge of Iron Age Britain was still in its infancy and therefore the error of confusing an Iron Age camp with one of Roman date may well be pardoned, though hardly on the grounds on which the error was based.

So what had changed to justify such a statement? Leeds' report on the excavations demonstrates the advances in archaeological techniques and thinking. The immediate difference is that there is a much firmer division between presenting the evidence and the excavator's interpretation of it. For the first time in Wychwood a scientific approach is taken to archaeological exploration.

The excavation report has a discernible strategy with a detailed statement about where the trenches were placed and why they were so positioned. The overall aim of the project was to place the date of the camp on a surer foundation, but individual trenches were placed to discover the form of the rampart, identify the shape of the gateways, and to compare the settlement within the camp and immediately behind the rampart with other known examples, in this case Chun Castle in Cornwall, an Iron Age fort which had been excavated in by Leeds in 1925-30. Each of the trenches is numbered and illustrated on an accompanying plan with exact details of its position in the text. Since 'there is no super-imposition of consecutive layers' no section drawings were included, but there is a lengthy description of what was found in each trench. When particular features were discovered, other trenches were dug to test any hypothesis that was suggested by those features.

Besides the attention to the detail of the plan of the site, which includes the composition of the sub-soil as well as structural features, the locations of artefacts are also considered. The objects unearthed, besides the pottery, were very few and these are analysed in terms of the material of which they were made: bone, stone and metal, and the dimensions given. A bone comb was the only artefact that was distinctive and the excavator was able to draw on a growing corpus of examples from other sites and conclude that while it was not a common type, it had a wide distribution throughout the whole of the United Kingdom.

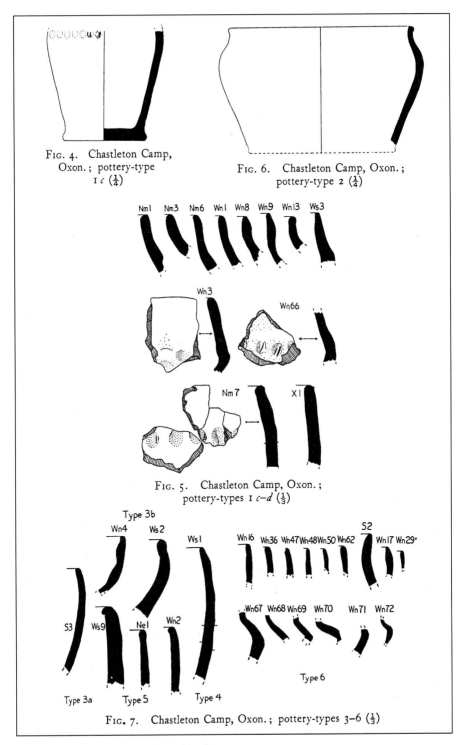

FIG. 4. Chastleton Camp,
Oxon.; pottery-type
I c ($\frac{1}{4}$)

FIG. 6. Chastleton Camp, Oxon.;
pottery-type 2 ($\frac{1}{4}$)

FIG. 5. Chastleton Camp, Oxon.;
pottery-types I c–d ($\frac{1}{3}$)

FIG. 7. Chastleton Camp, Oxon.; pottery-types 3–6 ($\frac{1}{3}$)

3.5 Pottery from Chastleton (Soc. of Ant.)

The innovative aspect of the excavation report in terms of previous work carried out in Wychwood was the analysis of the pottery found. The fabric, the physical constituents, were isolated into types and the treatments applied to the fabric were identified; in this case none of the sherds indicated wheel throwing and only a few had been burnished by polishing or rubbing. The form, or shape, of those vessels which could be re-constructed was divided into categories: a bucket shape, wide-mouthed vases of squat form, bowls or cups and fairly tall vases. In each category examples are described and the museum, in this case the Ashmolean, accession numbers of outstanding examples are given to enable future re-examination. Often a vessel is cross-referenced to another similar type found at excavations elsewhere in the country. Examples of rim-shapes are illustrated and the decoration applied to the pots is analysed: fingertip, finger-nail, linear and wavy-edge. One sherd is identified as having no parallels in form or fabric from elsewhere in Britain in pre-Roman times and having been submitted to expert opinion it is suggested that it might have originated in Tuscany, thereby demonstrating trade in commodities from the Mediterranean.

The report uses the pottery as a means of dating the site, identifying the functions that took place there and determining how it was connected to other places. The site at Chastleton was placed in the wider context of the growing knowledge of the Iron Age in other parts of Britain and allowed comparison with other sites. This use of typology enabled archaeologists to suggest that pottery forms were distinctive enough to be compared with groups of people in the Iron Age. The recognition of forms that originated in Europe gave rise to the idea of successive invasions and mass movements of social groups to Britain. This is important in understanding Leeds' conclusions.

Having laid out the evidence, Leeds draws three main sets of conclusions. Firstly, the findings of the 1881 excavation, that occupation of the camp was of short duration, are confirmed. Secondly, the pottery suggests an early Iron Age date and the limited number of forms supports the limited time span of occupation. Finally, the wider implications of the excavation are considered. The Midlands lagged behind the coastal counties in the reception of new influences from the Continent, though it was impossible to suggest whether the infiltration of new peoples had been swift in a conquest, or through slow advance. Leeds preferred the slow infiltration option, with pioneers belonging to the first stock of newcomers having moved so far forward as to carry them beyond the immediate range of new influences, and so having retained their original culture unmodified by changes which were in progress in their rear.

The pottery at Chastleton is, as has already been remarked, undistinguished. It has all the appearance of belonging to a ceramic phase approaching its last gasp, and in its unmixed character may be sought an explanation for the brief active life of what must have been a fortification of considerable strength.

In the forty-three years between excavations at Chastleton huge leaps forward had been made both in technique and in knowledge of the Iron Age. Leeds' work links Wychwood with the rest of Britain, and suggests a process whereby the area was colonised by Iron Age peoples. Today, the idea of successive waves of colonisation from Europe is not in vogue, and changes in the archaeological record, for example the development of metal working or pottery styles, are seen as the results of far more complex and deep-rooted social processes which cannot be explained simply by the arrival of new people. However, it is upon the work of archaeologists such as Leeds that such sophisticated interpretations have been built.

1935: Radford and Ditchley Villa

Another of the important developments of the post-First World War period was aerial photography. In the early part of the 20th century air-photographs had been taken from balloons and the first known air-photographs of archaeological sites were taken of Stonehenge in 1906. However it was the 1914-18 war that saw the development of manoeuvrable aircraft and the skills that were to realise the full potential of the technique. Aerial photography was a completely new method of archaeological exploration by which buried features could be traced through differential growth of surface vegetation, most readily seen from the air. Crop marks as such were not entirely unknown before this from ground observations and had even prompted excavations, but these were isolated instances and had not prompted any general conclusions leading to a search for other examples.

O. G. S. Crawford was one of the pioneers of British archaeology. He was using distribution maps of finds and sites before the First World War and he introduced the air-photography of earthworks shortly after it. His publication of *Wessex from the Air* in 1928 defined a new archaeological approach which we now take for granted. The book was produced in collaboration with Alexander Keiller, the 'marmalade king' and patron and explorer of the Avebury prehistoric circle site. When they served as airmen in the First World War – Crawford as an observer and aerial photographer in the Royal Flying Corps and Keiller in the Royal Air Service – both had been struck by the way that quite familiar earthworks could look different from the air. An article in the *Observer* on Stonehenge brought the two together. Keiller put up the money, the RAF provided an airfield and the de Havilland company provided the aircraft. It was a risky business taking photographs from the air. The photographer leant out of the open cockpit and often to get the right picture the plane had to fly at such an angle that there was just time for him to do so before the plane developed a spin. Crawford became the founder of the journal *Antiquity* and Archaeological Officer to the Ordnance Survey ensuring that ancient monuments were recorded in the cartographic record. We owe the fact that sites are still shown on maps available to the public to his determination.

Crawford undertook fieldwork on the Grim's Ditch, and the implications of Crawford's view of this feature for our understanding of the past of Wychwood will be examined in a later chapter. He had an enormous influence on archaeological fieldwork, not least in seeing landscapes as a unit for enquiry as opposed to individual sites.

One of the people influenced by Crawford's work was Major George W. Allen whose interest in aerial photography was fired in 1930 by a casual read of one of Crawford's Ordnance Survey publications in a hotel in Southampton. Allen was by profession an engineer and director of his family's firm in Oxford who undertook air photography in his leisure time. As a person of independent means, though with no previous archaeological experience, he was at liberty to fly where he wanted. Allen sought out promising places within a twenty-five mile (40 km) range of his Oxford home base and flew over the same site as often as he thought warranted, the first time that an area so rewarding had been observed at all seasons over a period of several years. For nearly ten years before his death at the age of forty-nine in a motor cycle accident, he discovered hundreds of sites in the Oxford region.

Crawford and Keiller had relied on accidental observations or brief 'one-shot' missions, but Allen sought not only to discover and illustrate archaeological sites of all kinds, but also to understand the processes that brought them into view. He photographed the same site at different seasons to demonstrate its varying appearance, and took a closer look at crop marks by examining them on the ground. An expert solo flier, he piloted his plane, a Puss Moth based at Kidlington, and often designed and built his own cameras using his engineering knowledge. Allen tended to stress the use of oblique views, which Crawford spurned. He photographed the Ditchley villa in 1934 and the following year demonstrating his superb use of the oblique view in a magnificent set of photographs of the crop marks and subsequent excavation of 1935 .

The site of Ditchley Villa had been known since at least 1857 when Jordan published his *History of Kiddington* and observed that it was 'thickly strewed with stones… broken brick or tile, with some occasional remnants of pottery'. In 1867, Colonel Lane-Fox had uncovered a pavement, probably on this site. However, it was not until 1935 that an excavation of the site was mounted and the villa became a 'classic' in Romano-British archaeology, although it contained neither a hypocaust system nor mosaic pavements. The excavation was carried out by

3.6 The excavation of Ditchley villa. (Ashmolean Museum)

C. A. Ralegh Radford who studied Modern History at Oxford and graduated in 1921. His experience as an excavator before Ditchley included work at Whitby Abbey, after which he travelled to Czechoslovakia and Venice and then became a student at the British School in Rome and subsequently, Athens. During the latter part of the 1920s he worked on the excavations at the Richborough Roman site. From 1929 until 1934 he was Inspector of Ancient Monuments for Wales and Monmouthshire and his series of guidebooks to many of the Welsh monuments were to survive for nearly 30 years. In the period before he took up a post as Director of the British School in Rome, Radford, who preferred to be known as a West Country man, was publishing papers on Roman signal stations in Devon and the Scilly Isles and excavating at Tintagel, Ditchley and with Sir Mortimer Wheeler in Brittany. Whilst many of the conclusions of his subsequent excavations were later shown to be wrong, he nevertheless was a pioneer whom others followed. He died in January 1999 at the age of 98 years.

The broad aim of the excavation was to solve 'some of the problems connected with the Roman villa system' and work took place over ten weeks in the summer and autumn of 1935. Since Allen's photographs indicated the plan of the villa, they also dictated the method of exploration. In order that the dimensions of the villa complex could be accurately measured, narrow, long cuts were made and it soon became clear that blank areas on the photograph contained no remains as the soil was so thin as to show up all the detail from the air. In order to establish the sequence of the various features revealed and to recover sufficient objects to date the different building periods, extensive excavation of the main structure was undertaken.

The main building of the villa proved more complex than had been first thought, especially with the removal of later building collapse revealing earlier structures on the same site. Through the identification and recording of the complex stratigraphy of the site, three building phases were isolated and for the first time in the Wychwood area, earlier timber structures were recognised. This information was recorded on a general plan and in a number of drawn sections through the site enabling study and reconsideration by future archaeologists.

In the published report, these sections and the accompanying plan are referred to constantly in the description of the excavation of each room and area. Although the site had been badly damaged by ploughing and little remained above floor level, photographs of the excavated remains were taken to show rela-tionships between the features. The result is a comprehensive description of each area, the soil changes, structures and the location of finds. The careful observa-tion of the stratigraphy and the structures of the site enabled Radford to draw detailed conclusions about the nature of the structures above foundation level. The use of pottery and coins associated with particular layers and areas, especially Samian ware which had been imported from the Continent and was particularly amenable for dating, aided the elucidation of the structural phases and use of the buildings.

Radford went on to excavate the rest of the villa enclosure, identifying a threshing floor, a well, a southern building and granary, the enclosure wall and its gate and the roadway that left the villa through it. It was the completeness of the excavation that was so staggering for its time, and Radford was able to use this data to build up a convincing picture of the development of the villa and its economy, including the fact that it had not been demolished or destroyed but had been allowed to fall into decay.

The excavation was very competent when compared to earlier attempts to explore the Roman villas of the area. Radford's excavation deserves to be noted because of its contribution to the understanding of Roman villas as dynamic structures over long periods of time and the complexity of the activities imme-diately around them. Radford also used Allen's photographs to try to reconstruct the farming regime immediately around the villa but with limited success. He also attempted to quantify the amount of grain the granary might have held and its implications for the amount of land needed and possible populations. However, there was a lack of attention to animal bone that was recovered yet is

3.7 The site of the Cassington complex today. (Author)

not represented in the report. This was rectified in Thomas' excavation of the Callow Hill villa complex less than a mile to the east in 1950 and the work at Shakenoak in 1960–7. One of the most far-reaching results of the excavation was to show the efficiency and effectiveness of aerial photography as the site had acted as a test bed for the technique.

1931–1951: The Cassington Tragedy

To see the record of archaeological research in the Wychwood area as one of progress only would be misleading as there have also been set-backs, such as the destruction of the Cassington prehistoric complex. A flooded gravel pit, marked on present maps as Marlborough Pool (SP 453103), but better known to archaeologists as Smith's Pit II and Tolley's Pit, marks the site of the destruction of an archaeological landscape of immense importance with sites from the Neolithic period to Saxon times. In 1931 the A40 Oxford -Witney road and Cassington by-pass destroyed the site of a Romano-British cemetery and part of an Iron Age site. In 1933 an aerial photograph (see page 68) showed a great sub-circular enclosure and circle complex. The Iron Age 'Big Enclosure' was completely destroyed by gravel quarrying in Smith's Pit II and now flooded as Marlborough Pool. Between 1939 and 1951 some 20 separate salvage excavations and observations were undertaken in Smith's Pit II by almost every archaeologist working in Oxford, many of which remain unpublished. The large enclosure ditch itself of some 700 metres (2300 feet) was narrowly sectioned in only five places. Only one

3.8 Aerial photo of Lee's Rest taken by Major Allen. (Ashmolean Museum)

entrance of the three known was closely examined and evidence of the internal structures contemporary with the enclosure ditch is non-existent. Although a great deal of archaeological excavation was carried out, it was executed in a piece-meal fashion over a long period. It is impossible to reconstruct the layout of the human elements in the past within the Cassington complex. Today, this would not have been allowed to happen and a very strong case would have been made for the preservation of the Cassington sites. At the very least, a rescue excavation of the total area would have been considered a necessity.

1960–1992: Allen, Linington and others at Lee's Rest

On 5th June 1933 and 1st October 1934, Major Allen flew over the Charlbury and Stonesfield areas and took a number of photographs of rectangular crop marks which he thought were traces of Roman period structures. He identified and photographed triple enclosures about a mile south-west of Ditchley, in a field where there was a spring immediately north-west of Lee's Rest Farm, east of Charlbury. Parts only of the ditches were visible, because a plantation made since 1889 had obscured the remainder, but the internal measurement was about 55 feet (16.7m) square and the external 220 feet (67m). Later fieldwalking produced potsherds of 2nd to 4th century date and the evidence as a whole was thought to indicate a farm.

The site remained uninvestigated by excavation until June and July 1960 when over the period of a fortnight the Oxford University Archaeological Society, under the direction of R. E. Linington, sampled the three ditches and a small area in the interior of the enclosure outside the bounds of the plantation.

Linington became interested in archaeology as a schoolboy when he worked on the excavation of Lullingstone Roman Villa in Kent. At Oxford he read Physics at Pembroke College and became President of the Oxford University Archaeological Society. The excavation was probably the first occasion when what is now known as geophysics was employed in the Wychwood area. Linington's interest in the application of scientific and geophysical techniques to archaeology prompted the use of a proton magnetometer to locate the ditches and proved particularly useful within the plantation and saved much labour. Since the excavation has never been published in full (Linington died in Rome in 1983, an international expert in geophysical prospecting) these points have never been explained further or illustrated by the use of plans.

The Lee's Rest site was not very exciting in terms of the structures located and examined as many of these had been badly damaged by ploughing, but the finds indicated that something unusual had occurred during the time of the change of use. Finds from throughout the occupation of the site appeared to be mainly associated with agriculture. However, the number of small bronze objects recovered suggested a religious use and this was further supported by the recovery of a small stone head, possibly from a statue of Mercury. Linington postulated that during a third-century reconstruction of the site, in addition to the more normal farming usage, some shrine or other building with religious associations had been present on the site. In his summary report Linington suggested that this interpretation was borne out by 'some unusual aspects of the planning of the interior at this period'.

The site itself was not investigated further until the 1990s but in the intervening period many finds of bronze objects and coins were recovered by individuals using metal detectors and this reinforced the notion of a religious rather than purely agricultural site. In 1992 tree felling in the plantation provided an opportunity to map the uncertain boundaries of the enclosure using magnetometry, which would have pleased Linington. The project was undertaken by the Ancient Monuments Laboratory of the Historic Buildings and Monuments Commission for England to assist the future management of the site.

Of the various geophysical methods available, magnetometry was selected because the clayey subsoil over the Great Oolite limestone brash was more amenable to this form of prospecting. It had also been used on a number of Iron Age sites elsewhere and had a proven record of locating occupation features. An alternative method, resistivity, was rejected because of the potential disturbance

of the site by tree rooting and water-logged conditions.

The survey was carried out in two areas which were divided into a grid of 30m (98.4 ft) squares. Each square was then surveyed to record the vertical magnetic field gradient at intervals of 25 cm (0.8 ft) along successive parallel transverses 30m (98.4 ft) long and 1m (3 ft) apart. The data was downloaded into a portable computer and later processed in a laboratory to produce the final plan. At the same time magnetic susceptibility readings were obtained in the laboratory from samples of top soil collected at 15m (49.2

3.9 Magnetometer survey at Lee's Rest. (English Heritage)

ft) intervals along a 135m (443 ft) traverse crossing the enclosure from east to west. The purpose of this technique was to get an indication of the intensity and distribution of any past settlement activity associated with the enclosure as burning can convert naturally occurring iron minerals in the top soil to more strongly magnetised forms. The samples were sieved to get rid of unwanted inclusions and measurements were taken using among other things a Bartington susceptibility bridge that was made by a Charlbury company.

The results from the magnetometry survey showed that the enclosure is roughly symmetrical and square in form, and that the ditches are interrupted on the southeast side by a possible entrance causeway. The corners of the innermost circuit of the ditches was more sharply angled than the outer more rounded two. It proved impossible to locate the outer ditch on the north-west side which may be incomplete or local factors may have hindered its discovery. In places the signal from the ditch had been obscured by clearance bonfires which gave a strongly magnetic response and may have included modern iron debris. Within the enclosure it proved difficult to identify ancient features or even the evidence from the trenches of the previous excavation. However, slight evidence was recovered for occupation features outside the enclosure. The results of the magnetic susceptibility survey indicated that any previous occupation may not have been of an intensive or sustained nature.

However, the Lee's Rest site does define some of the characteristic of the evolution and problems of archaeology of this period in the Wychwood area. The site was discovered from the air and some fieldwalking took place before an excavation was undertaken. As is often the case, the excavation was never published in full and the finds have been dispersed so that they cannot be re-examined. Inevitably over time the remains of the structure have been damaged by ploughing and to a small extent finds have been removed by metal-detector users. However, even though inconclusive, modern non-invasive geophysical techniques have added to our knowledge of the form of the buried feature. Clearly, further work needs to be carried out at Lee's Rest before a more definite identification of its function will be possible.

1992: The Cotswold Archaeological Trust at Deer Park Road, Witney

In October and November 1992 a salvage excavation took place on the western edge of Witney in advance of house building on the site. In 1991 the Planning Policy Guidance Note 16 (PPG 16) issued by the government had extended the concept of 'the polluter paying' to damage to historic sites which meant that the developers, Bovis Homes (South Western) Limited, had to provide funding and resources for an excavation by the Cotswold Archaeological Trust. PPG 16 was to changed the face of British archaeology in many ways, not least by ensuring that threatened archaeological sites were evaluated and, if necessary, excavated. In an age aware of the fragility and scarcity of natural resources, this represents a major change in attitudes towards the evidence of the past, the human cultural resource, as threatened, important and non-renewable. The Witney Deer Park site was to be one of the first sites to benefit from the new legislation.

An earlier evaluation of the site in November 1991 had revealed previously unknown middle-Iron Age activity in the form of postholes, surfaces and ditch alignments. The main aims of the excavation were to recover the plan of the site, date it and understand its main characteristics. Topsoil was stripped by machine in two main areas and the archaeological features revealed were then hand excavated. The excavation took place in the wettest November for 50 years and the weather became a severe constraint on what could be achieved.

Graeme T. Walker, who led the excavation, was a member of the Cotswold Archaeological Trust based in Cirencester. The Trust is indicative of the way that archaeology had been organised since the 1970s with dedicated units undertaking professional work rather than the exploration of the historic environment being organised on an ad hoc basis. Walker had been with CAT since taking an archaeology degree at Reading University with a special interest in prehistoric sites. Previously he had completed an HND in Practical Archaeology at Dorset Institute of Higher Education, a course which indicates new routes into archaeology and its growing professionalisation. Later he was to be elected a Member of the Institute of Field Archaeologists, another indication of how the profession was policing standards and of the position of archaeology as an important aspect of the planning process.

The excavator was able to determine from very shallow archaeological features that had suffered from ploughing and sparse finds that the site had been an undefended farmstead with two distinct areas. One, Area A, was domestic in character and the other, Area B, a general utility area where a range of activities took place.

The excavation report shows the complexity of a modern excavation and various scientific disciplines that are involved in a modern excavation. The pottery was sorted into its main fabric types and weighed to suggest how many vessels might have been present. Each fabric was examined microscopically to see the constituents and to compare them with pottery from other local sites. Dating of the pottery was supported by radio-carbon dating of charcoal from the round-house gully and indicated a date of 350–115 BC. Radio carbon dating had developed since 1949 and measured the decay of the radioactive isotope C14 . It provides a dating source independent of archaeologists' judgements. Iron slag was analysed and suggested blacksmithing activity. The worked stones were subjected to geological analysis and their origins pinpointed. The economy and the state of the surrounding land was suggested by an analysis of animal bones and seeds and pollen.

The planned and meticulous excavation of this small site, even in atrocious weather conditions, demonstrates the way that attitudes to the past and the techniques for recovering evidence have changed over the last decades. Deer Park Road, on the edge of the Wychwood area, is an example of what modern excavation and research can achieve in the on-going and developing discovery of Wychwood's past. Even small and heavily degraded sources of evidence can be made to produce a complex picture of what was happening in a location two thousand years ago. What is also important is that such a low-status site was even excavated and this points to the recognition of the need to understand the whole landscape and not just those sites that will produce wealthy or artistic objects.

Overview

The case studies show an increasingly sophisticated approach to collecting evidence and its interpretation. Reading opinions of early antiquaries and historians about past life in Wychwood may appear strange to us, but we need to take into account the limited frameworks for the interpretation of evidence with which they were working. They were very much exploring a 'new' world. Through time the techniques for identifying and retrieving the evidence have become more increasingly sophisticated and the questions asked of the evidence influenced by the attitudes of society.

Many Victorians saw Roman villas as evidence of a successful imperial people similar to themselves and drew distinctions between the Roman dignitary in his villa and the 'native' British. Today we are more likely to see the influence of Romanisation on the Iron Age peoples who adopted Roman lifestyles, an important aspect of which was the villa way of life. We do not know that North Leigh villa was not lived in by a general from Rome, but our experience of colonisation elsewhere in the world in the recent past causes us to interpret the evidence as the results of colonial influence acting on a local population. In a more equal and fair society we are also interested in how the ordinary people, who might have worked in a villa settlement, lived as much as the owner's living conditions. This influences excavation strategies in that questions are asked about areas around the villa and we are concerned to locate the low status non-villa settlements that must have existed to support the villa with a work force.

New techniques, often developed in other disciplines, have also widened the range of questions that can be asked of structures, artefacts and ecofacts. Today a wide variety of experts examine the evidence retrieved from archaeological sites and it is possible to place a site in both its human and natural context, giving us a much more complete picture of the activities that took place in a particular location in the past.

There can be no doubt that our understanding of Iron Age and Roman Wychwood has benefited from the area being near Oxford University. However, our knowledge of the development of the area in the past is still very sketchy. There has been little advance in our understanding since the small-scale research campaigns of 1930, the 1950s and 1960s and any re-interpretation of the sites has been largely due to work elsewhere. The Thames Valley, conversely, has been the subject of intensive archaeological activity mainly due to its propensity to produce many more well defined cropmarks and to the threats from gravel quarrying which have been prefaced by salvage excavations, often paid for by the extractors. From this research we are already aware that during the period 700 BC to 500 AD the formation of alluvium in the Thames Valley grew in pace, no doubt

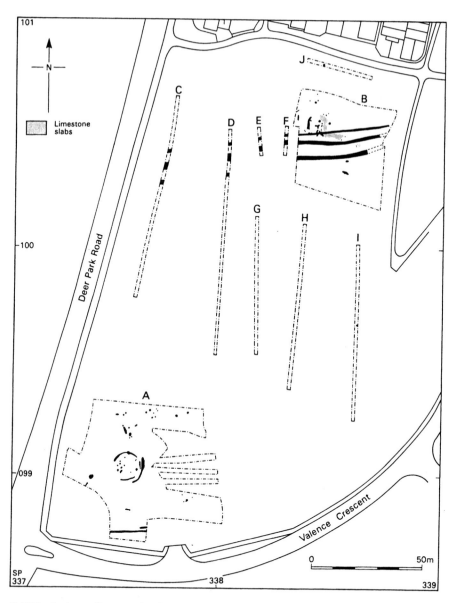

3.10 The features discovered at Deer Park Road, Witney. (OAHS; *Oxoniensia* 60,72)

a result partly of expanding agriculture in the Cotswolds and Wychwood. Conversely, whatever happened in Wychwood during the period must have been influenced by the agricultural activity in the Thames Valley and there may have been greater interdependence than we can guess at now. Perhaps one of the greatest tasks for the future, besides identifying new sites, will be to link the economies of the two areas.

4

The Early Iron Age
(800–400BC): The Hillforts

The Early Iron Age might have been marked by the more frequent use of the iron rather than bronze but it is the huge social and economic changes which were already happening that are of greater significance. One of the major changes was the gradual expansion of farming in response to a growing population, though the Wychwood area, an insecure border region, was probably less densely occupied and peripheral to the Thames Valley. With agriculture being increasingly important there would have been efforts made to prevent land stealing and cattle rustling which could have been responsible for the growth of hill forts and the development of political territories. The larger population would also have led to an increased need for social control and food which could have resulted in the development of a social hierarchy with chieftains increasing their power over the local population. The growth of such a hierarchy might have been a contributory factor in the need for defendable settlements, though the hillforts that appeared in Wychwood in the late sixth and fifth centuries bc need not have been central places of power dominating and overseeing a peasantry. They would have been built to protect the local inhabitants in case of attack, as many of them would have lived outside the enclosure in a landscape dominated by hamlets or small villages. No doubt power waxed and waned and about 400 BC many of these early forts were abandoned.

Hillforts are enclosures with ramparts built to protect settlements or stock. The 'hillforts' in the Wychwood region are a misnomer, as only two of a possible eight, Round Castle and Ilbury, actually correspond to the popular image of a contour fort where the ramparts circle the highest point of the contrasting relief of the south Wychwood area. Eynsham Park Camp, Idbury, Lyneham Roundabout and Chastleton Burrow are better described as plateau forts built on flat ground with no natural advantage of any kind and their tactical strength being provided by the defences. With the exception of Eynsham Park, they are situated on the high, even land of the Cotswold dip slope. The possible forts at Knollbury and Bruern (if either or both are of this date) are on valley sides of the rising Cotswold dip slope, over-looked and without any strategic military position or strength of construction. They were not constructed for defence but more likely as stock enclosures. There is an absence of defended enclosures in the central part of the region around Ditchley and Cornbury though this does not necessarily mean a lack of population in these areas or that they were covered with woodland though both are possibilities. This lack of hillforts does indicate that in times of conflict the inhabitants would have not had the possibility of a haven close by and this perhaps suggests a small population.

What little evidence we have from excavations at Lyneham and Chastleton suggest occupation in the sixth and fifth centuries BC Both consisted of a single bank though only at Lyneham was it possible to suggest the detail of its construction. An U-shaped ditch about 7 feet (2.13 m) deep fronted a rampart that was revetted by dry externally and internally. The rampart had a core of small Oolite slabs and prob-ably had a vertical outer face and sloping inner side and might originally have been about 6 feet (1.82 m) high. No trace of a palisade was found surmounting the rampart but an accumulation of large stones might indicate the presence of a paved rampart walk. At Chastleton no traces of an external ditch were detected and the rampart material might have been derived from stones collected locally. However, the presence of charcoal flecks among the Oolite blocks of the external face of the wall may indicate the presence of a timber-faced rampart.

Chastleton had two opposing entrances, with the pillar-like stones possibly forming part of a gateway. At Lyneham only one gateway survives, evidence for the opposite one having been destroyed by quarrying. The form of the defences in both cases appears to have been the work of one building episode. This lack of modification indicates they were little changed throughout time and therefore appear not to have developed during their use and so it is likely that they were occupied only for a few centuries. Few of the other local forts have been surveyed and several have been subjected to ploughing and quarrying making it difficult to ascertain the detail of their construction. Some, such as Eynsham Park or Round Castle survive in woodland, which again makes diagnosis of their features difficult.

Of two of the forts that have been partly excavated, the strategy was focused on the defences, so it is impossible to say with any certainty what occurred inside them. From evidence of early hillforts elsewhere it would appear that they were built on or close to sites which had already become focal points in the landscape. They appear to have been occupied by communities practising a normal range of domestic activities. Hearths, pottery, a possible shale bracelet and bone objects, including a bone comb and needles as well as a spindle whorl which may indi-cate the presence of sheep, were found just behind the bank at Chastleton. They may not have been occupied continuously but perhaps seasonally or in times of social conflict. At Lyneham no traces of occupation were found which might

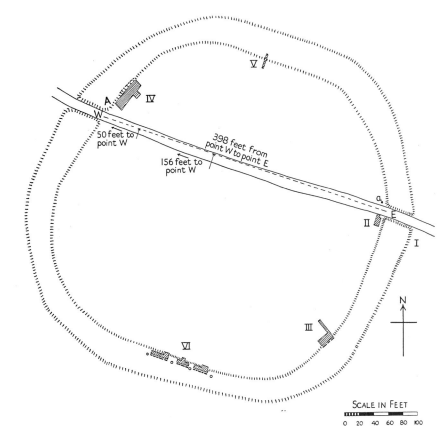

4.1 Plan of Chastleton Camp with Leeds' excavation trenches. (Soc. of Ant.)

indicate that the enclosure was associated with pastoral agriculture, but very little of the interior has been inspected. At Round Castle hardened, reddened clay in the front of the rampart suggested burning of timbers but whether this was accidental or by deliberate conflict is difficult to say.

The hillforts

Chastleton Barrow   SP 258282

A plateau fort from which the land falls gently in all directions to give good all-round views. Its shape is sub-rectangular and encloses about 1.4 ha (3.5 acres). The defences are covered with trees and scrub and consist of a single steep-sided bank standing about 3 m (10 ft) above the interior and 4 m (13 ft) above the exterior. There is no definite sign of a ditch and with the present height of the banks it is unlikely that it could have been filled by rainwash or collapse. The interior has been much ploughed. The present opposing entrances are probably original.

4.2 The rampart at Chastleton Camp. (Author)

Excavated in 1881 and 1928–29, some evidence for Early Iron Age occupation was found. The site is further discussed above and in Chapter 4.

Hill Farm, Bruern   SP 244175

A possible hillfort with ditches and banks measuring 120m (396 ft) by 90 m (297 ft) with a possible entrance on the long side to the south. The earthworks are well marked out on the ground and the bank and ditch are 15 m (49 ft) to 18 m (59 ft) across and the bank up to 9 m (30 ft) in width. The site has produced Roman and medieval pottery.

Eynsham Park Camp   SP 394113

A plateau fort and annexe forming two conjoined enclosures 122m (400 ft) above sea level, the one to the north is sub-circular in shape and has univallate defences enclosing 1.4 ha. (3.5 acres) and is covered in woodland and game stocked. The entrance is to the south-east. The bank remains up to 1.5 m (5 ft) high and the ditch 1.5 m (5 ft) deep. There is good visibility though the defences are of major strength especially on the north where visibility is marred. There is no evidence of the collapse or mutilation of the defences and at present the whole is in excellent condition. Two cuttings through the ditch in 1955, the results of which remain unpublished, produced no dating evidence. Pollen retrieved from beneath the rampart indicated the presence of oak woodland prior to the construction of the hillfort. To the south is the larger rectangular enclosure of 3.2

4.3 The bank at Knollbury. (Author)

ha. (8 acres) generally clear of trees. It has a bank up to 1m (3 ft) high with traces of an exterior ditch but no evidence of occupation. The southern enclosure was not intended for defence as it is over-looked especially from the east. Both elements may be of a different date but contemporaneity is assumed.

Idbury Camp   SP 229195

A roughly circular plateau-fort at 198m (650 ft) above sea level with land falling away to both west and east and good all round views and univallate defences enclosing c.3.6 ha. (9 acres). The enclosure was permanent pasture until 1940s when as a result of war time contingencies it was ploughed and this has continued until the present day so that is now no longer visible. There were traces of a counterscarp on the northern side and the entrance was possibly at the north-west. In 1980 fieldwork identified the rampart as a band of yellow limestone compared with dark chocolate brown soil inside the camp and lighter cocoa coloured soil on the outside.

Ilbury   SP 438305

A pear shaped contour fort from which clayey slopes fall away in all directions, most steeply to the west. The enclosure covers c.2.4 ha. (6. acres) and had univallate defences, most of which has been ploughed out. Air photographs suggest an entrance at the south-east.

Knollbury   SP 317230

A gently sloping site roughly rectangular, 150 m (429 ft) long and 100 m (328 ft) wide enclosing about 1.4 ha. (3.5 acres) with its longer axis across the contour, N.W.-S.E. It has a single steep-sided turf covered bank up to 3m (9.8 ft) high, and highest at the northern end, and Oolite rubble and signs of a revetment of larger

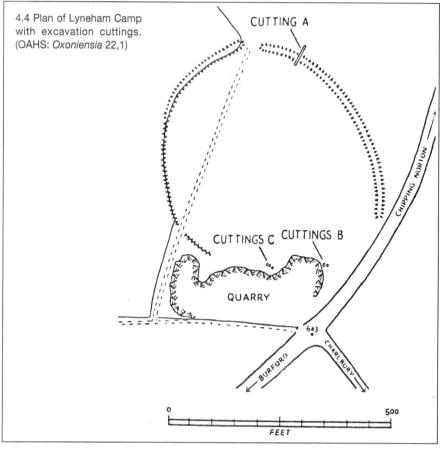

4.4 Plan of Lyneham Camp with excavation cuttings. (OAHS: *Oxoniensia* 22,1)

CUTTING A

CUTTINGS C CUTTINGS B

QUARRY

CHIPPING NORTON

643

BURFORD

CHARLBURY

0   500

FEET

limestone slabs. There is no evidence of a ditch and the interior is higher than the exterior. No dating evidence has been recovered and the interior has been ploughed. It is most likely to have been a stock corral.

Lyneham Roundabout   SP 299214

A roughly circular plateau fort with good all-round views and enclosing 1.75 ha. (4.33 acres). Its univallate defences are in parts destroyed or lowered by a road, quarrying and a plantation. The bank is best preserved on the north west where it rises to 2 m (6.6 ft) above the interior, but the ditch is only visible on the west. The original entrance is probably the gap at the north. The interior has been severely ploughed. The defences were examined in 1956 and the results are discussed above.

Round Castle   SP 457138

The site is covered in trees and in a poor state of preservation. It is of oval shape measuring about 1 ha. (2.5 acres) and about 35m (115 ft) above the

4.5 The northern entrance at Lyneham. (Author)

surrounding countryside. On the south and west sides is a double bank while on the east and north only a single bank and ditch, though embanking in later periods makes this unclear. The rampart is made mainly of clay with dump lines of sand faced with stone walls some 6 m apart. There is burnt clay in the rampart. At the rear of the rampart in places there is evidence for collapse sealing some 20 cm (0.6 ft) of soil and two successive pebble surfaces that abutted it. From this soil horizon Early Iron Age pot has been retrieved.

The wider landscape

While it is possible that these forts represent a stage of the developing process of controlling the land by a controlling group the relationship of the hillforts to the landscape is harder to gauge. In other areas of south central Britain, the process of control of the land is emphasised by the appearance of linear ditch systems and droveways which may have staked out territorial boundaries. In the Wychwood area the evidence for this process is lacking at present, though no doubt territories did exist and were inhabited by a population engaged in farming. Two of these farming settlements, one at Rollright and the other at City Farm, Hanborough have been explored and indicate that at this time wide spread woodland clearance had already occurred on the Cotswolds. From work in other areas of south central England we can surmise that cattle, sheep and cereals were important, particularly hulled barley and spelt and that manuring probably took place.

5

The Middle Iron Age
(400BC–100BC):
Banjos and Other Settlement

Banjo Enclosures

The development of aerial photography has enabled us to identify aspects of past landscapes that can't be seen from the ground. This is particularly true of boundaries such as trackways and ditches that edged fields. Recent research has demonstrated that large areas around Charlbury and Enstone were devoted to fields in the Iron Age, but unfortunately the necessary very dry summer conditions that allow this type of mark to show in the crop are very infrequent and few have occurred since the recognition of the boundaries. The opportunities for viewing this type of evidence are further restricted by the planting of crops that are not susceptible to cropmarking such as oilseed rape, peas and root crops. However once aerial archaeologists and researchers became aware of the possibilities a number of landscape features were identified from older photographs including several enigmatic enclosures know as 'banjo enclosures', because of the similarities between the plan of these monuments and the shape of a banjo.

Up to a dozen banjos are now known in the Wychwood area, almost all situated on the limestone plateau mainly around Enstone, Kiddington and Wootton. However the distribution extends as far as Dustfield Farm in Charlbury where Middle Iron Age pottery has been recovered from the surface of the site. It may be significant that their distribution is in an area which contains no hillforts and perhaps they are indicative of settlement of previously wooded land in response to growing population.

Banjo enclosures seem to have originated in the Middle Iron Age. They were first recognised in Wessex and appear to be very common in some areas of Hampshire, Dorset and Wiltshire. Now increasing numbers are being identified in the Upper Thames Valley, particularly in the Wychwood region. Banjo enclosures comprise of a central area and are small, circular, ditched enclosures of less

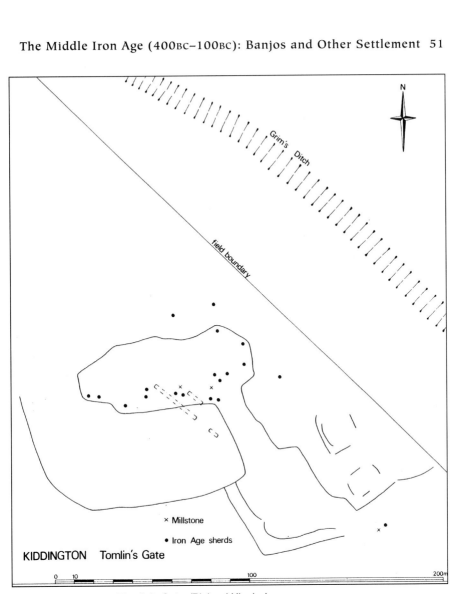

5.1 Banjo enclosure at Tomlin's Gate. (Richard Hingley)

than 1 hectare (2.5 acres) and are approached by a long causeway defined by ditches on either side. They do not seem to be defensive in the military sense, but might perhaps have protected against predators or dangerous animals. They are usually found on hillslopes and valley sides, though not on steeply sloping ground. They were originally thought to be cattle enclosures but the few examined by excavation have produced evidence of domestic occupation continuing to the Late Iron Age.

Recent studies of banjo enclosures indicate that most, if not all, were settlement sites with elaborate entrances. It has been suggested that the long approach must have had a specialist function, possibly providing a facility for some aspect of animal husbandry such as gelding, shearing, branding or slaughtering.

Excavations within the central enclosure of several banjo enclosures have revealed a variety of elements suggestive of fairly widespread and intensive occupation. Storage pits, likely to be for cereals, are probably the most encountered feature. Gullies presumably served as drains. Recorded structures, mostly represented as groups of post-holes, include round-houses, gateways and fences. Since in some areas they are succeeded by Roman villas, it has been suggested that banjo enclosures were settlements of some status which were in the hands of the minor elite. Barry Cunliffe excavated the central area of a banjo extensively at Nettlebank Copse in Hampshire. He found evidence for a Middle Iron Age date for the laying out of the enclosure on an earlier habitation site. However, the banjo appears not to have been used significantly during this period. In the Late Iron Age the corridor and enclosure ditches were re-dug and the banjo continued in use possibly for seasonal feasting and ritual activities.

The best known banjo enclosure in the area is at Tomlin's Gate in Kiddington, lying on a slightly north-west facing slope. It appeared on Allen's aerial photographs in the 1930s but it was not until 1980 that Richard Hingley sectioned one of its ditches. The ditch enclosure was located and appeared to contain a series of re-cuts indicating a long life. There were no finds from the site but fieldwalking produced some quantities of pottery clustering over the enclosure and of Middle Iron Age date (400–100 BC). To the west of the trackway forming the neck of the 'banjo', and bounded by it, there appear to be a number of paddocks unconnected with the central enclosure or trackway. They appear to be interconnected by way of gaps through the slighter earthworks of which they are formed.

Interestingly the Tomlin's Gate banjo is close to a section of the Grim's Ditch. Usually the course of the Grim's Ditch is on the crest of the highest ridge in the area, though at Tomlin's Gate it is in fact below the crest of the ridge in front of the banjo which occupies the highest ground. The implication of this is that the Grim's Ditch was respecting the banjo. If the Ditch was constructed in the first or second quarter of the 1st century AD as is generally accepted, then the banjo must still have been in existence and functioning at that time.

Unenclosed settlements

Aerial photography indicates that not all of the settlements of this period in the Wychwood area were enclosed, though we have little idea of their morphology. Excavations on unenclosed settlements have not taken place within the core of Wychwood, but at Deer Park Road in Witney in 1992 part of such a settlement was carefully excavated.

In one part of the site, Area A (see Fig. 2.1), the remains of a round-house were recovered. It was surrounded by gullies which were probably designed to shed water from the roof of the house and collected household rubbish and had to be cleared several times. The house appeared to have a front entrance with two posts, one for a lintel and the other from which the door was hung. There was also a rear entrance. Inside were pits that were interpreted as cooking holes and contained charcoal, a broken quern for grinding corn, and pottery. The lack of any stake holes around the perimeter of the house led the excavator to assume that turf had been used for the walls.

Two smaller structures were postulated from postholes and hearths around the roundhouse, possibly a small roundhouse or basic shelter. Other hearths may have been set against a fence line for protection from the wind in this exposed place. A water trough or cistern was also found with post holes around it which might represent protection from animals. Close-by a slab lined pit containing burnt limestone may have been a cooking or roasting pit and iron objects were found in its fill that suggested the remnants of a roasting spit.

In Area B was an extensive L-shaped area of paved limestone around which were distributed seven shallow hearth pits which gave the impression of a purposefully organised working area, as if the pits were serviced from the pavement. The amount of oak charcoal compared to burnt cereal remains indicated a non-domestic purpose for the area. A small gully contained three fragments of iron slag and these were interpreted as concerned with the manufacture or repair of tools, though they could have resulted from just one day's blacksmithing.

The types and amount of pottery found at Deer Park Road suggested that the site was not in use for very long and it could be broadly dated to from around the 3rd century BC to the end of the 2nd century BC. This date was supported by radiocarbon dating of charcoal from the round-house gully which indicated a date of 350–115 BC. The evidence recovered suggested that the processing of harvested cereals and repair of iron tools probably took place in the fields or paddocks around the site, and therefore the evidence from the excavated site was not representative of all the activities that happened in the immediate area.

The worked stones found on the site were querns, used for the grinding of corn and other food materials. Surprisingly, the stone came from May Hill in Gloucestershire, some 65 km (40 miles) from Witney. This raised the problem of how the stone was transported, whether by land or river, and whether there was a trading pattern involved.

Although bones did not survive well on the site due to the nature of the soil, cattle, sheep/goats, dog and pig were identified, with cattle being the most represented, though large bones survive better in these conditions. Charred plant remains were examined using a binocular microscope to identify wheat and barley as well as the seeds of black medick, blackberry, dock and goosegrass, with rose and sloe or hawthorn also represented in the remains. This gives an idea of the economy and the state of the surrounding land.

The hillforts

In the Middle Iron Age in other parts of central southern Britain, some hillforts were strengthened or enlarged and these developed hillforts emerged as central places. In the Wychwood area there is no evidence of any increasing complexity in the structures of the known hillforts and what little artefactual evidence we have suggests that they were abandoned by this time with the inhabitants of the area living in non-hillfort settlements. The vast majority of these have yet to be discovered.

6

The Late Iron Age (100BC–AD43): The North Oxfordshire Grim's Ditch

The North Oxfordshire Grim's Ditch or Dyke which dominated the Late Iron Age landscape of Wychwood, is an enigmatic feature. The origin of its name, which means the Devil's Ditch, suggests that this has been so since at least the Saxon period. The Saxon inhabitants clearly did not have a conception of projects which involved massive earth moving and named a number of linear prehistoric monuments throughout southern England to indicate supernatural origins. To differentiate the Wychwood example from these several Devil's Dykes or Grim's Ditches, the appellation 'North Oxfordshire' is usually used.

The first mention of the Grim's Ditch was in a charter boundary of 1005 near Long Hanborough *than on on haethfield on tha ealdan dic* ('then on to the open heath to the old dyke'). Another stretch in what is now Ditchley Park was used to define the remaining forest area in 1300 in the *Perambulations of Wychwood*:

'And so from Dicheleye straight along the hedge running between the land of Henry of Dychele and the land of Agnes of Bloxham to the aforesaid Grimesdiche in Dicheleye'. Ditchley means 'the field of the Ditch'.

The extent of the Grim's Ditch

The North Oxfordshire Grim's Ditch is a series of banks and ditches enclosing about 80 square kilometres (30.9 square miles, 8000 ha., 19,789 acres) between the valleys of the Glyme, Evenlode and Windrush in the parishes of Charlbury, Spelsbury, Enstone, Glympton, Wootton, Woodstock, Hanborough, Freeland, North Leigh, Ramsden, Finstock and Cornbury.

The extent and continuity of the ditch structure have been the pervasive aspect of research up until the present. However, it is unlikely that we will ever be able to recognise all the aspects of the Grim's Ditch as erosion and human destruction throughout its post-use history make examining the linear aspects of the earthwork difficult. Agriculture and quarrying have flattened or removed large parts of the evidence of the system. These processes were observed by the Reverend J. Jordan, vicar of Enstone, in his 1857 parish history:

> In order to render it more subservient to the plough the escarpment has been considerably lowered, and the material, of which the boundary was formed, has been spread over the ground it encloses. The work thus done, under our eyes at the present time, tells us how in previous ages, at other points of the course of this boundary, the same process of demolition has gone on, and will account for the absence of it altogether at certain intervals.

The integrity of the earthwork system was first proposed in O. G. S. Crawford's paper 'Grim's Ditch in Wychwood, Oxon.' in *Antiquity* in 1930, where he designates it 'The Wychwood Grim's Ditch, North Oxfordshire'. Although various antiquarian observations had linked elements of the ditch, especially between Blenheim, Ditchley and Charlbury, it was Crawford who first suggested the continuity of the earthworks south of the Evenlode with those to the north of the river. He considered that it had been a continuous boundary with any gaps being due to later destruction. While other, later, commentators have interpreted the gaps in the course of Grim's Ditch as having been filled with woodland or marsh and doubted Crawford's assertion, the earthwork features he identified are still accepted today.

His paper is worth examining in detail as it demonstrates his logical and methodical way of working. First he presented the problem: 'Nothing absolutely is known of the age or purpose of any of these [other 'Grim's Ditches' throughout Southern England] ditches... the Wychwood Grim's Ditch has been the least known and the least studied. Hearne walked along part of it; and obtained from a farm labourer, a "elderly man" of Ditchley, the valuable information that it continued from there to Charlbury, Cornbury and Ramsden "where it joins Akeman Street".'

'When, therefore, I began to investigate Grim's ditch in Wychwood, the known portions consisted merely of a sector a mile and three quarters in length running through Ditchley Park and of two discontinuous fragments of a total length of a mile in the woods between Ditchley and Wootton... It was evident that the fragment in Blenheim Park was a southern portion of it.' He also noticed an 'intrenchment' marked on the map half a mile south of the village of North Leigh running east and west for 700 yards (640 m). Crawford set out to try to join up all these elements into a much greater whole.

His exploration began on the south side of the Evenlode. 'I had gone to Ramsden Heath to look for the remains of a certain 'hulwerke' last heard of many centuries ago.' (A typically thorough footnote details the various ancient spellings of the name in medieval documents.)

6.1 The Grim's Ditch at Ditchley House. (Author)

As I was bicycling along the road, in a field on the south side I saw the angle of an old bank and ditch protruding from a field hedge. I though at first that it would turn out to be a moated enclosure of medieval date; but on inspecting it I found that it continued more or less in a straight line in both directions from the angular point, connecting up with the 'intrenchment' already marked on the map.

A photograph, taken in 1933, in his autobiography shows him dressed in heavy coat, flying helmet and fur gloves, holding a bicycle the handlebars and cross bar of which are draped with maps.

His doggedness is evident as he further describes his efforts;

Naturally the tracing out took several days; and even when I had done all I could on the ground there still remained a gap of a mile between Poffley End and Singe Wood, where the remains of it seemed lost. The gap was filled by observation from the air. Flying along it for this purpose, I observed a broad band of darker green corn crossing a field diagonally, and continuing (as a mark of some kind or other) to the western end of Spicer's Lane. I flew along this sector on several different occasions and satisfied myself that what I saw was the authentic Grim's ditch. Then I went along the ground again. But there I could see nothing, even though I now knew exactly where to walk. Even the broad green line in the corn was totally invisible from below.

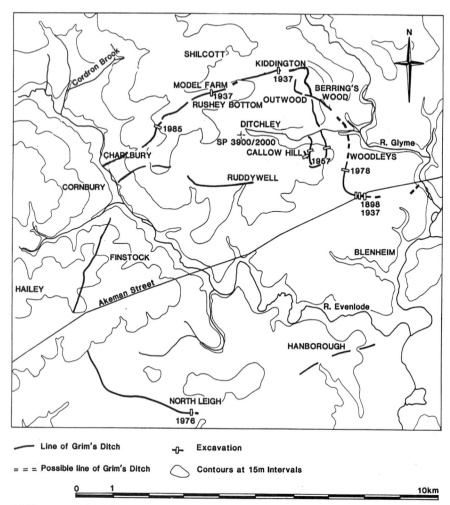

6.2 The extent of the Grim's Ditch. (Adapted from OAHS: *Oxoniensia* 53, 280)

It is unclear whether Crawford undertook the flying in between fieldwork in the same season or returned when the crop was at the same stage in growth in a future season. However, he seems to have been flying on his own as no photographs exist from this episode, though his personal library was destroyed in an air raid on Southampton in the Second World War.

His observations are always sharp. Looking for the ditch near the Shepherd's Hall pub on the Witney to Bladon road,

> I noticed from the air a broad band running parallel to the Witney road at a distance of about 100 yards south of it. The field is under grass and was then laid up for hay: but apart from an ancient field boundary and a belt of ragwort in flower, I could see nothing on the ground.

He also worked around Blenheim tracing that stretch as far as Outwood. He notes the best preserved stretch in Blenheim Park 'here it has never been disturbed and the top of the bank is about seven feet above the bottom of the ditch'.

It was fifty years before the next full survey of the Grim's Ditch system. During the 1980s and 1990s Copeland investigated the preservation of the elements identified by Crawford and, through the use of aerial photographs and an examination of all the documentary evidence relating to the features, a number of new stretches of earthwork were identified and visited on the ground. This was the first occasion that aerial photographs, many taken in the 1930s and during World War Two, had been used to define the course of the ditch north of the Evenlode. It was soon clear that the ploughed out elements of the ditch were showing up as either crop or soil marks and that it was possible to define the course of the ditch over long stretches.

As a result of the survey at least two continuous stretches of the earthworks in between the Evenlode and the Glyme were suggested. One can be shown to have run uninterrupted by major breaks from the Callow Hill area, where a number of dykes had been previously identified, through Ditchley to Charlbury. The second continuous element climbed from the Glyme, through Blenheim and on to Outwood where it seems to stop, perhaps unfinished. A third, shorter element climbed the Evenlode valley east of Charlbury and seems to link with other known stretches continuing back towards Callow Hill. South of the Evenlode, it appeared that the ditch ran from in the vicinity of Finstock church through North Leigh to a point above the Evenlode near Long Hanborough. Since the landscape between North Leigh and Long Hanborough was largely pastoral, and in places heavily wooded, it was not possible to demonstrate the continuity of the earthwork, though it does appear to be discontinuous, probably the result of its never having been completed. This was confirmed in 2000 when a water pipeline was laid across the course of the Grim's Ditch at several points. Neither east of the present upstanding section at North Leigh nor between Finstock and the Evenlode could any trace of it be located.

The stretches of earthwork between Callow Hill and Charlbury and Blenheim and Outwood seem particularly well adapted to the landscape. Both have the characteristics of riding the crest of the ridges over which they travel, always keeping to the highest ground available. The short stretch east of Charlbury does climb the landscape very efficiently in part but its known highest reaches tend to veer away from the most appropriate route and the ridge is in front of it in places. This stretch is unusual in that its ditch faces into the area of the main enclosure rather than away from it as is characteristic of the other stretches north of the Evenlode. It is possible that this element is an internal feature, perhaps to form a 'funnel' with the other element to the west, or of a different date.

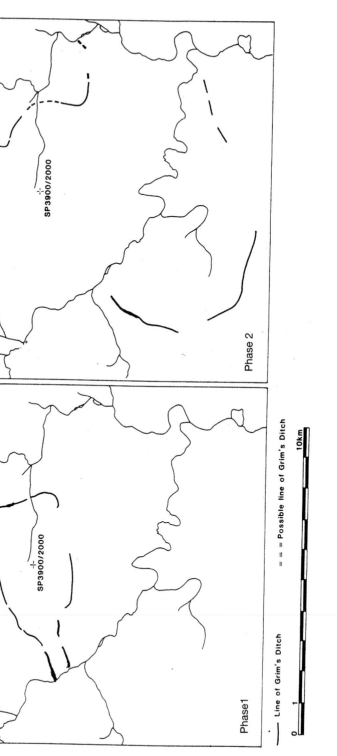

6.3 The phasing of the Grim's Ditch (OAHS: Oxoniensia, 53, 282)

The profile of the Grim's Ditch

Crawford's assessment of the Grim's Ditch prompted a number of excavations across the line of the earthwork in 1935-6 at Ditchley, Kiddington and Blenheim. These were followed by sections at Callow Hill in 1950, North Leigh in 1975 and Charlbury Quarry in 1985. The results of these excavations showed that there was a similarity in the construction of the earthwork across the various stretches but also a variation in its dimensions due, probably, to different work gangs constructing separate parts of the ditch, possibly at different times. The bank varies between 6 metres (19.7 ft) and 13 metres (42.6 ft) in width with a ditch in front of it of about the same dimensions. The ditch is invariably about 1.5 metres (4.9 ft) deep and, since the bank is clearly upcast from the digging of the ditch, this also was presumably the height of the bank. There is no evidence for a palisade on top of the bank, although traces of its bedding trenches may have been eroded over time. Between the bank and the ditch is a berm, an area of flat ground, between 1.5 metres (4.9 ft) and 3 metres (9.84 ft) wide. The ditch is always on the outside of the sequence. Where excavation has been extensive enough to detect it, a trench about 50 cm to 75 cm (1.6 ft–2.5 ft) wide and up to 25 cm (0.8 ft) deep has been identified in every excavated section, except one at Callow Hill, between 3 and 6 metres (9.84 ft–19.7 ft) from the ditch edge, possibly forming an outermost feature of the sequence and interpreted as a palisade trench forming a fence-like feature of unknown height. Unfortunately, it has not been possible to recover stratigraphic evidence to demonstrate that the palisade trench is contemporary with the bank and ditch.

The date of the Grim's Ditch

The Saxon derivation of the name is valuable in that it does give us a date before which the features must have been constructed. Before archaeological excavations took place, the absolute dating of the construction of the Grim's Ditch had the subject of varied opinion. Dr Plot (1677) thought it Roman, as did Jordan (1857) and Lane Fox (who later became that celebrated archaeologist, General Pitt-Rivers) in 1869. Warton (1783) considered it to be Iron Age though he admits 'it is difficult to determine by whom or when it was made'.

The earliest archaeological work to take place on the ditch system was by Professor Haverfield in 1898 at the intersection with Akeman Street in Blenheim Park. Haverfield suggested that the Roman road had cut the pre-existing Grim's Ditch structure. Crawford derided Haverfield's work;

> This entrenchment makes a sharp turn eastwards exactly at the point where it crosses the Roman road, Akeman Street; it was here that the late Professor Haverfield excavated it. The ground here has been much

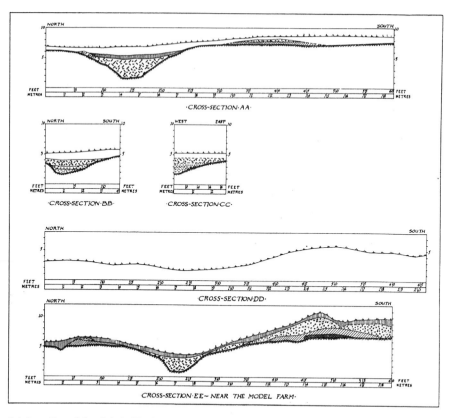

6.4 A section of the Grim's Ditch at Model Farm, Ditchley in 1935-6. (OAHS: *Oxoniensia* 2)

disturbed, so that excavation might be expected to prove inconclusive unless carried out with a finesse that was almost unknown in those days…in any case it was inconclusive and had better be forgotten. Apart from anything else, the sharp bend strongly suggests that the Roman road was already there when the ditch was made.

Crawford had already made up his mind before beginning his fieldwork that 'For topographical reasons it seems impossible to doubt that the Wychwood Grim's ditch was made by the Romano-Britons'.

Earthwork features are notoriously difficult to date as material in their banks and ditches might well be residual from earlier structures that have been destroyed during construction. However, within a few years of Crawford's paper, the excavations on the line of the Grim's Ditch in the Ditchley, Kiddington and Blenheim areas were to show that it was a pre-Roman Conquest feature. The trenches cut across it in the 1930s and 50s produced forms of Iron Age pottery from below the bank and early Roman pottery was found low in the filling of the ditch which indicated a pre-Roman date, probably in the first half of the first century AD. The evidence suggested that the Grim's Ditch was late Iron Age.

The excavation also identified that in the Ditchley-Kiddington and Callow Hill areas the ditch was deliberately back-filled soon after it was dug with material from the bank being cast into the ditch. However, the Blenheim sections showed that the ditch had silted naturally. Copeland suggested that there was a correspondence between these finding and his proposed two continuous stretches north of the Evenlode. He postulated a relative chronology for the earthwork system with two phases in the construction of the Ditch (see Fig 6.3). The Callow Hill-Charlbury sector, Phase One, was constructed first, and having being back-filled, was succeeded by the Glyme-Outwood section, Phase Two, which had probably never been completed. Since both phases had similar dimensions and cross profiles it was likely that only a short time passed between their successive constructions. Corroborating evidence for this proposal appears to come from an aerial photograph taken over Outwood in 1935 by Allen, where the phases were to seen to intersect with the Glyme-Outwood section cutting, and therefore later than, the Callow Hill-Charlbury element.

The only section though the Ditch south of the Evenlode, at North Leigh, showed that it had silted naturally, but at the present time there is no way of ascertaining whether the Phase Two earthworks north and those south of the Evenlode are contemporary, though Copeland postulated that they were of the same period.

If the various earthworks which are designated as the North Oxfordshire Grim's Ditch are of broadly the same period and are part of a unified design, at their most expansive they would have enclosed about 80 sq. kilometres (30.9 square miles, 8000 ha., 19,789 acres). The earliest phase might have been designed to demarcate a triangular area formed by the courses of the Evenlode and Glyme and enclosing the catchment area of the stream that runs south of Ditchley. Later the area demarcated might have been expanded to focus on the Evenlode itself with the earthworks stretching from Ramsden to Long Hanborough intended to form the southern boundary. This would emphasise the importance of water in a largely limestone area.

The function of the Grim's Ditch

Dr Plot suggested that the Grim's Ditch was a branch of Akeman Street probably because of its intersection with the Roman road in Blenheim Park. Warton in his Kiddington parish history suggests that it was a boundary, probably between Iron Age tribes, though he does consider that it might have been constructed to hinder the advance of the Romans, 'but that it was a boundary, and not a road, certainly not a Roman road, the irregularity of its course, and its confirmation, are sufficient evidences'. Lane Fox (1869) used his military experience in assigning a strategic function to the feature; 'it is not merely a boundary but without doubt a fortification, for its commanding position, its adaptation to the features of the ground, and the situation of its ditch, are points to which, viewed tactically, are sufficient to determine it to be a work of defence'. Permutations of these early opinions have surfaced continually in the later analysis of the feature.

The most elaborate, and fantastic, explanation of the purpose of the Grim's Ditch was constructed by Crawford (1930). There is something almost Tolkeinesque about this tortuous proposal and the maps accompanying Crawford's text would not have been out of place in *The Lord of the Rings*. He saw it as a late Roman structure: 'Presuming in Roman times there was a native track or ridgeway leading from here to the Cotswolds, these barriers would effectively check the progress along it of an invader who might have been held up in his attempt to enter the region by way of Akeman Street'. For a man who had survived the First World War and had been used to see 'intrenchments' hold up armies, it was a natural progression to see Grim's Ditch in the same light. He also noted that there were a number of villas around the area. He used the conception of the natural vegetation from his Second Edition of the Roman Britain Ordnance Survey map ('areas of natural woodland have been restored upon a geological basis') to postulate a tongue of forest land projecting southwards down the Evenlode Valley from the Great Midland Forest which separated the villas of the Cotswolds and North Oxfordshire. This hypothetical stretch of woodland nearly met the forest of the Upper Thames valley but just failed to effect a junction. A natural 'pass' is left through which went Akeman Street uniting the two populous districts. He is even more precise: 'The Pass of Wychwood, as it may be called, is situated between Charlbury and Bladon. More precisely it lies between Fawler and Bladon bridge, now called Hanborough bridge'. The area within the Pass of Wychwood was grass and light scrub with occasional trees in open formation without undergrowth. 'It was easy country to travel over in primitive times and must have provided good hunting, good grazing or good arable land, according to the needs of its inhabitants'. It was this route that the Saxons would have used to get to villas of North Oxfordshire and then pass on to those of the Cotswolds. Therefore, Grim's Ditch was a defensive frontier to protect the late Roman villas.

Once the Ditch had been assigned to the late Iron Age, ideas for its function, inevitably, coalesced around the Roman invasion and Harden, in 1936, suggested that it was constructed to halt the Roman armies' progress. Thomas (1956) agreed with this possibility but also suggested that it might have been a defence thrown up by a tribal group, the Belgae, who were accessing the territory of 'native Iron

Age folk' and needed the security of the earthworks. Harding (1972) preferred the option of a period of 'cold war' between Iron Age tribes in the period before the Roman Conquest as the setting for the construction of the ditch. He saw the ditch and its gaps, possibly incorporating tracts of forest and marsh, as ideal for chariot and mounted guerrilla warfare.

We are more aware of the nature of tribal expansion today and consider the River Cherwell and the Grim's Ditch area as the boundary between the Catuvellauni to the east and the Dobunni to the west, largely based on coin evidence. Today the Grim's Ditch is generally accepted as being in Dobunnic territory, though recently Eberhard Sauer suggested that the Grim's Ditch, being largely westward-facing, was the boundary of the Catuvellaunian lands west of the Cherwell and part of a defensive system including Ave's Ditch which runs from the vicinity of Kirtlington to near Ardley and possibly beyond. The main argument against Sauer's conception is the different styles and profile of these separate ditch systems.

Clearly, the Grim's Ditch took a great deal of effort to build, requiring more labour than can have come from the known settlement inside the dyke. This is particularly so if the palisade trench was part of the feature as it would have been deep and wide enough to hold timbers of considerable thickness and height. If it was in existence around the whole feature an enormous amount of timber must have been used in its construction. In the absence of settlement within the area demarcated by the ditch work gangs must have been drawn from a large area around it. However, without any evidence for the chronologies of individual sections, there remains a possibility that it was constructed over long periods of time by relatively few people. Since its construction must have taken a considerable amount of time it is unlikely to have been a response to the Roman invasion, which probably saw Roman troops in the area just a few years after the conquest of AD 43. More likely the function of the Grim's Ditch was political, social or even possibly religious, or a combination of all three.

Copeland suggested that though the earthworks north of the Evenlode were particularly well adapted to the landscape, the Grim's Ditch was too long a feature to be manned effectively, and too slight a barrier to act as a defensive or strategic barrier. While the earthworks might exclude, particularly if the palisade trench was an integral part of the feature, this exclusion was more likely to be for social or economic reasons than for warfare. It would seem that some powerful individual, or group of individuals, had caused the construction of the Grim's Ditch, but perhaps the fact that it lay on a tribal boundary and contained a number of religious shrines, indicated that it was a central place of a particular grouping of Iron Age people, possibly the eastern group of the Dobunni.

6.5 Crawford's map of the Grim's Ditch. (*Antiquity*)

The factors in favour of such an economic or social function are persuasive. Grim's Ditch is positioned at the junction of major cross-country routes. The Meareway or Saltway, a likely prehistoric routeway that runs in a north-west/south-east direction and cuts through the centre of the ditch system on its way to Stonesfield and beyond. Akeman Street, which is possibly pre-Roman, also crosses from south-west to south-east joining to important Iron Age tribal sites at Bagendon (Dobunni) and St. Albans (Catuvellauni). It has been proposed that the area acted as a 'gateway' between the Trinovantes (to the south) and the Dubunni, but not enough coin evidence exists to prove it. David Miles has suggested that it was the 'kraal' of the Dobunni, and used in the movement of cattle from the less developed areas to the north and west to the more prosperous south.

At the present time, little Iron Age settlement has been located within the Grim's Ditch system, though evidence for this period is particularly difficult to locate on the ground and is absent from air photos. The Grim's Ditch has evidence of Iron Age settlement below its banks at a number of points, and there was evidence of a settlement focus at Callow Hill where hearths and occupation were found inside enclosing ditches. Some indications of Iron Age occupation were found below North Leigh and Shakenoak villas and there are two examples of banjo enclosures within its bounds. At Lee's Rest Linington interpreted the two inner ditches of the three being constructed in the early first century AD. He thought that only the inner ditch, which had a bank along its inner edge, had been left open, while the other one was used as the foundation of a palisade trench. The whole sequence of palisade, ditch and bank seemed to have formed the boundaries for structures in the enclosure. This combination reflects that of the Grim's Ditch and the site may have a close relationship with it. Outside the confines of the ditch large areas of possibly Iron Age fields have been recognised in recent aerial photographs, indicating a marked contrast to the land inside. However, without evidence of settlement it is difficult to assign any firm function to the monument.

A tribal *oppidum*?

It is unlikely that the purpose of the Grim's Ditch will be identified through close examination of its earthwork features alone and it is necessary to look for other examples of land marked out with linear earthworks elsewhere that might offer parallels to its function. Archaeologists in recent decades have identified large-scale settlement complexes, *oppida*, which were often surrounded by substantial but discontinuous dykes. They appear to act as a focus for their regions, and represented major communal efforts which indicate a measure of social centralisation. At one extreme was a complex, multi-functional site such as Camulodunum, present-day Colchester, with separate areas for religion, craft activity, settlement and perhaps the residence of the tribal elite. At the other end are sites like Stanwick in North Yorkshire which are equally as extensive, though less densely settled, but with evidence for both craft activity and settlement. Some 'enclosed' *oppida* developed at the beginning of the first century AD, such as Salmonsbury in Dobunnic territory, and had mostly been abandoned by the Roman conquest. Others such as Stanwick and Bagendon (Gloucestershire, also Dobunnic territory) came to prominence after AD 43, due to their location on the frontiers of the newly established Roman province. These latter are often known as 'territorial *oppida*'.

The increasing permanence and importance of tribal organisation in the late Iron Age defined an increasing role for its leaders and enhanced need for a tribal

CASSINGTON.

6.6 The Big Ring at Cassington taken by Major Allen. (Ashmolean Museum)

focus. This focus may have developed in a number of ways. An elite settlement may have formed the nucleus around which a centre grew, and this seems to be the case at Bagendon and is possibly the usual pattern. Alternatively, the sites may have begun as temporary or periodic meeting places, perhaps even in a normally unoccupied and neutral location – for example on the edge of a tribal territory. This function as a place where the clans came together allowed the development of ritual functions where the gods oversaw the activities and were provided with shrines. This coming together at a meeting place further encouraged the development of trade activities; meanwhile clan and temporary tribal leaders may have maintained normal residence at their rural home bases. Whether or not permanently occupied, the focus of the tribe became identified with the central location and a number of functions became established. The place symbolised the tribal identity, acting as a communal centre as much as the focus for any particular individual. Only if there had been a powerful elite or individual need would the centre have combined the symbolic with the residence function to become a tribal town. *Oppida* were extensively involved in long-distance trade with the Roman world; in several cases, their rulers had probably entered into formal treaties with the Emperor.

It is likely that the Dobunni were a loose federation of tribes and a number of tribal centres have been identified; Bagendon, Salmonsbury near Bourton on the Water, and Dyke Hills at Dorchester are well distributed and might represent the sub-tribal organisation. It is possible that the Grim's Ditch was also a tribal centre, an *oppidum*, at the edge of the Dobunnic territory. Although no elite residences have yet been identified, it is possible that they lie either under large Roman villas such as Stonesfield or in areas which have a high density of woodland. Evidence for religious activity or cult centres has been discovered in Blenheim Park and may exist around the later Roman site at Lee's Rest. The Iron Age religious practices related to water, particularly pools, might also a find a focus in the pool at Spurnell's Well in Bottom Wood, Ditchley, which is a sheltered and flat area ideal for settlement, but unavailable for research due to timber cover.

The first of Copeland's proposed two phases may well represent the development of such an enclosed oppidum in the second quarter of the first century. If this was the case, it might be expected that the response from contact with the Roman world would have engendered early signs of Romanisation and perhaps some indications of Roman monitoring of activities within the area.

The possibility that the Grim's Ditch was of growing importance for trade and commerce in the Roman conquest period will be discussed in the next chapter, when for the first time contemporary historical evidence will come into play.

Cassington Mill Big Ring

At Cassington, 5 km. (3.1 miles) south-east of the Grim's Ditch, is an unfinished Iron Age enclosure on the eastern bank of the Evenlode covering 5.3 ha. (13 acres). The site was destroyed by gravel-quarrying between 1938 and 1951. It was surrounded by a broad V-shaped ditch 10 metres (32.8 ft) wide and between 3 m and 4 m (9.8 ft – 13 ft) deep whose fill showed that a massive gravel bank had stood on its inner edge. There were at least two gaps in the ditch, one in the north east and the other to the south and probably represent gateways. Air photographs show a maze of interior features – pits, ditches, sub-circular and rectilinear enclosures. It has been assigned to the Late Iron Age with two structural periods. The first, dated by finds to the 1st century BC or 1st century AD, comprised the construction of the enclosure, after which its fortifications were allowed to silt into the ditch without any repair. The second phase, dated to the second quarter of the first century AD, saw the repair of the defences, which were levelled almost immediately afterwards. The ditch was allowed to silt naturally during the Roman period and the immediate post-conquest period seems to have been prosperous. In the absence of systematic excavation, the history and function of Cassington Big Ring has to remain obscure. It is possible that the earlier phase was constructed in response to the Catuvellaunian threat of the early 1st century. The

6.7 Grim's Ditch at Model Farm (Author)

second phase has been attributed to the Roman invasion, though this is unlikely considering its rate of advance and the possible friendly relations between the Dobunni and the Roman state. However, it has been suggested that the massive defences might be due to it being held by Catuvellaunian interests on the tribal boundary with the Dobunni. If so, the Roman invasion would have been a considerable threat to its occupants.

Interestingly, circular sites of the same dimension as the Big Ring have been identified to the north, at Little Tew, and to the east at Tackley, both at about the same distance from the Grim's Ditch. Whether this is fortuitous or planned is unknown at present.

7

The Roman Conquest

In AD 43 the army of the Emperor Claudius landed on the south coast and began its invasion of Britain. The actual landfall is the subject of dispute. It has been traditionally ascribed to Richborough in Kent, but recent discoveries indicate that a site near Fishbourne in Hampshire might also have been another beachhead. The invasion started slowly with Plautius, the commander of the Roman armies, having to search out the enemy, but eventually he defeated Caratacus and then Togodumnus, sons of the recently deceased Conobelinus, king of the Catuvellauni. Dio Cassius takes up the story: 'The Britons were not in fact independent but ruled over by various kings. With these two put to flight Plautius secured the surrender on terms of part of the Bodunni tribe who were subject to the Catuvellauni'. It has long been suggested that 'the Bodunni' was a scribal error for the Dobunni. It seems likely that a detachment of the Dobunni would have been ordered to support the Catuvellaunian group against Plautius. However, rather than risk being involved in such a confrontation, the leader of the Dobunni decided to seek out the Roman commander and sue for peace.

This action may have allowed the ruler of the East Dobunni, whoever it was, to have been a 'client king' of the Romans after the conquest. Rome was quite accustomed to establish land frontiers against barbarian peoples, and they had adopted, from their earliest expansionist period, a simple but highly effective device – the client relationship with a carefully selected local ruler. The Emperor accepted the king or ruler as his client after his submission, *deditio*, and thus assumed that the subjects of that ruler in turn were held then in the same state of independence. By this means, Rome secured an outer buffer to her frontiers with little effort and expense. The main object of the treaty terms, which defined a bond of *fides*, would have been to oblige the ruler to protect his territory against barbarian attack from without, and the Emperor would have agreed to assist his client in the event of a serious invasion or an internal revolt, perhaps by stationing a garrison on the edge of the territory for protection.

The legions and their accompanying auxiliary regiments fanned out and in a few years, perhaps a decade or so, most of the lowland area of what is now

England was claimed as the province of Britannia. We are unsure which military units were involved in supervising the Wychwood area. It may have been a vexillation of Legio XIV Gemina which is thought to have struck west across the Midlands to the Welsh border where in the mid 50s it built a base at Wroxeter near Shrewsbury. However, since each legion had a large force of auxiliary troops as part of its command, it may have been several of these regiments that were responsible for the area. It is unlikely that the military presence would have been strong if the Dobunni had been friendly towards the Romans, though it might be expected that forts would be established on the boundaries of the territory to protect it from aggression (Dio Cassius states that a garrison was left in Dobunnic territory).

Roman military activity in the Wychwood area

A growing amount of evidence for early military activity in and around the Wychwood area has been found in recent years. This is very important as the early movements of the Roman army have been largely unknown due to the heavy cultivation of land in southern England destroying the evidence of forts and marching camps. Perhaps the most important new discoveries have been around Alchester near Bicester, long known to have been the site of a later Roman town. The site was first discovered by aerial photography in December 1990 when a 'playing card' shaped enclosure was identified. The date of the feature was also suggested by the finding of eight Roman coins in the area during the previous century. Further study of the aerial photographs showed a rectangular earthwork with a rounded south-western corner which is typical of a Roman military installation. Situated within the larger enclosure and using its southern ditch as part of its perimeter was another, smaller, rectangular enclosure. The Oxford University Archaeology Society excavated in the summers of 1996 and 1997 as well as carrying out a resistivity survey. The larger enclosure was found to have a V-shaped ditch typical of a Roman marching camp and previous finds of military equipment and brooches fashionable in the 40s-70s and two coins of the emperor Caligula (37-41) indicated an early date. The comparative frequency of early objects suggested to the excavator, Eberhard Sauer, that the camp had been the winter quarters for a detachment of the Roman Army. The camp was in an ideal position to exercise control over a wide area and to obtain sufficient food supplies for the winter.

The central enclosure appeared to be a raised platform with no structures inside it and no evidence of a gate. Its ditch was U-shaped which suggested it was not defensive in any way. This was interpreted as a parade ground for troops, raised off the rather boggy ground. The implications of this find were far-reaching as a temporary camp would not have required this facility. It suggested a more permanent fort close by. Sauer suggested that this fort may lie under the Roman town of Alchester which might have taken the two main roads in its northern half from the layout of the postulated fort. The discovery of a horse harness in the upper filling of a rounded ditch found in 1928 in the north-east of Alchester supports this idea. Further perusal of aerial photographs identified the western part of a rectangle with rounded corners west of the later eastern town wall. This indicated a further, very large fort possibly to house a thousand men.

These discoveries suggest that the area was an important strategic location in the early military occupation, being situated on the border of the Catuvellauni and Dobunni. The Alchester military complex is also sited at the crossing of the north-south road from Towcester on Watling Street to Silchester and beyond to the Fishbourne area with Akeman Street running from Verulamium (St. Albans) to Corinium (Cirencester). The pivotal siting of the fort to control these two important supply routes occurred early in the occupation, two timbers from the west gate having been dated by dendro-chronology (tree-ring dating) to October 44 AD–March 45 AD. The size of the largest of the Alchester forts indicates that it may have been a vexillation fortress, accommodating part of a legion with its auxiliary troops.

A marching camp, a temporary fortification for troops, was identified by aerial photography at Asthall in 1994. It was 0.85 ha. and was located on the south side of Akeman Street and aligned to it. The alignment of the camp leaves no doubt about the importance of the road, and suggests that Akeman Street had been laid out, if not actually surfaced, at an early date. There has been speculation about a more permanent fort in the area based on its locational position, where Akeman Street crossed the Windrush, and on the finds of part of a sword handle and pottery of early date. However, the evidence is very limited and not persuasive.

Further evidence of troops on manoeuvres has come from the identification of two rectangular marching camps near the Evenlode in Cornbury Park. These earthworks, previously thought to be prehistoric, are sited on rising ground on the western bank of the Evenlode in the north-west corner of the park. The Roman army habitually constructed defences for overnight stops, usually a deep ditch, a bank consisting of up-cast from the ditch and a breastwork defence made up of stakes carried by individual soldiers. Often these camps were thrown up as practice camps by troops on manoeuvres or on route marches. The Cornbury examples are unique in that they form one of the few places in southern England where above-ground evidence exists for the Roman army's activities. The lower of the camps has two rounded rectangular corners surviving. The west side is unfinished as is the north side. However, where surviving, the ditch is still 1.5/2m

(4.9/6.5 ft) deep and the bank 1/1.5 m (3/4.9 ft) high. The second, upper, structure appears incomplete with just the north and west sides and joining angle
traceable, though it appears to have undergone more erosion than the lower. It is
possible that both were built at the same time with the lower one being abandoned
in favour of the better view afforded by the upper one. Their unfinished state might

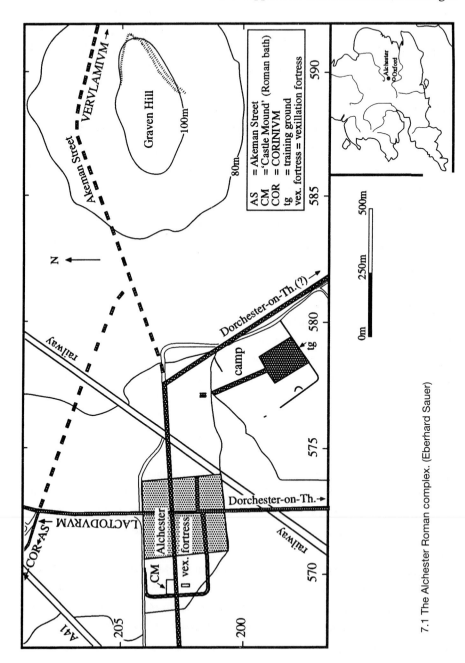

7.1 The Alchester Roman complex. (Eberhard Sauer)

AS = Akeman Street
CM = 'Castle Mound' (Roman bath)
COR = CORINIVM
tg = training ground
vex. fortress = vexillation fortress

be a result of the units involved practising only certain aspects of construction such as corners and ditches and that the camps were never intended to be complete. Undoubtedly both earthworks have survived because of the protection of the park environment and of never having experienced the damaging effects of ploughing.

The position of the camps is intriguing, just a few hundred metres south-west of the terminal of the Grim's Ditch in the Evenlode valley, though on the opposite bank. Was this an example of the Roman army demonstrating its power to build impressive earthworks in a few hours? Were these camps reminders of the presence of an occupying force in a largely unsupervised area?

Akeman Street

The role of Akeman Street in this early activity is difficult to ascertain. There is a case for seeing Akeman Street in the Wychwood area as a pre-Roman route across country joining the Grim's Ditch with Bagendon, and possibly St. Albans, as important centres for Iron Age communities. Early excavations in Blenheim Park where the Grim's Ditch and Akeman Street meet suggested that the Roman road was later than the earthwork, but this does not preclude the possibility that an earlier routeway on the same line may have been widened in Roman engineering activities. In this case Alchester would have been monitoring a road already in existence.

So insofar as the engineered road is essentially a Roman creation it may have joined a possible fort at Verulamium (St. Albans) with forts at Alchester and Cirencester. Hands suggested a date not later than AD 47 for the construction of an engineered Akeman Street, though it is very difficult to give such an exact date using archaeological evidence alone. The first fort at Cirencester does not appear to have been established until AD 50, and recent work around Cirencester, where there are datable contexts for the development of the city, indicate that the engineered Akeman Street was a later addition to the early road development, just before Corinium's street grid was fixed late in the 1st or early 2nd centuries. It is possible that an earlier course for Akeman Street left its present route at Barnsley in Gloucestershire to head towards Bagendon (there is an interesting lane called 'Welsh Way' which might be a suitable candidate). So any western terminus of Akeman Street is likely to be either at a site near Bagendon or an undiscovered fort site in that area.

It has been suggested that the Romans could have used Akeman Street to support a temporary frontier, a *limes*, whilst consolidating southern England. The finding of the fort at Alchester in a pivotal position strengthens this notion as does the location military activity at Asthall. The bow-shaped course of Akeman Street invites such an interpretation as it is a rather indirect route between Verulamium

Above: 7.2 The Cornbury Roman camps with the course of the Grim's Ditch on the slope beyond. (Author)
Below: 7.3 The corner of the northernmost camp. (Author).

and Corinium. If the Dobunni had the status of a client kingdom, this would have left a friendly tribe occupying the territory between Roman occupied areas and the River Severn and Midlands and makes the possibility of Akeman Street as a *limes* more attractive.

7.4 The Grim's Ditch and Akeman Street at Blenheim. (Author)

Grim's Ditch again

If Akeman Street was a Roman creation it was deliberately routed to pass near to the Phase One Grim's Ditch complex and the early importance of the area in the Roman conquest might give a new context to the Grim's Ditch. I have suggested that Phase Two of the Grim's Ditch is linked with the construction of Akeman Street and that Crawford was correct in suggesting that the earthwork in Blenheim Park was of Roman date, but early rather than later and built by the Dobunni rather than the invaders. The enclosed *oppidum* of Phase One became a 'territorial *oppidum*' covering a large amount of land and involved in trading.

Bagendon, a similar type of 'territorial *oppidum*' near Cirencester, is similarly placed in proximity to the line of Akeman Street and in the territory of the Dobunni, and has often been regarded as the tribe's central place. There is evidence that occupation at Bagendon continued for several decades after the beginning of the Roman occupation and it is possible that both Bagendon and the North Oxfordshire Grim's Ditch acted as economic 'funnels' for goods coming in from the west to the Roman-annexed areas of the south-east. At Wilcote, on Akeman Street, there is evidence of very early occupation, including imported pottery of a date in the reign of the Emperor Claudius and large amounts of animal bone. Hands, who has explored the Wilcote settlement, has identified a relatively narrow zone of activity little more than 30 m. (98.4 ft) wide on each side of Akeman Street. He has suggested that this settlement might have had a military origin and that its foundation might have been to provide a base for the road builders and later maintenance and as staging posts for military traffic using the roads. However, no objects linked directly with a substantial military occupation have been recovered.

The early Roman imported material and obviously local animal bone found by Hands at Wilcote could be interpreted as evidence for trading between the fledgling Roman province and the tribes outside it and the importance of the North Oxfordshire Grim's Ditch in this activity. There is also the phenomenon of some very early villas in the North Oxfordshire Grim's Ditch boundaries – for example, Ditchley and Shakenoak – and these might be explained by early proximity to Roman influence and possibly encouragement. The link is made much more likely by the finding of a type of storage jar, an amphora, with a specific carrot shape at Ditchley, Wilcote and Shakenoak. The form of amphora is dated to the early part of the Roman conquest and indicates long distance trade. Taking the argument further it is possible to suggest that the maximum development of the Grim's Ditch was a direct result of the Roman conquest and might even have had an important political role as a centre of the client king's power. This might offer a reason for the presence of the Roman army in the area in the late AD 40s, that of supervising or supporting the activity taking place in the North Oxfordshire Grim's Ditch.

What is clearer is that the influence of the Roman occupation was felt within a few decades of the conquest with the establishment of villa-like buildings at Ditchley and Shakenoak. It appears that the Iron Age communities were stable, wealthy and ambitious enough to have welcomed Romanisation at an early stage. We may also be seeing the continuance of a wealthy Dobunnic aristocracy with its lands intact, paying tax to the invaders and adopting the trappings of status under the new regime.

8

Akeman Street and its Settlements

The road network

In the changing landscape of the Roman period, one constant was Akeman Street, and in attempting to answer the question 'What was life like along Akeman Street?' much depends on which part of the period is being examined.

Akeman Street enters the Wychwood region at Sansom's Platt and crosses it north-east to south-west leaving it at Asthall. It was an important arterial route in the Roman period joining the *civitas* capitals of the Catuvellauni, Verulamium-St. Albans, and the Dobunni, Corinium-Cirencester. While Akeman Street has the characteristically engineered straight stretches typical of many roads of the period, its representation as a straight line across the countryside on Ordnance Survey maps is simplistic, and its actual course is often irregular in response to the rise and fall of the landscape and more clearly reflected in parish boundaries. The road has some spectacular features where it crosses some of the more entrenched features on its course. At Bagg's Bottom, south of Stonesfield, the road, after having crossed the Evenlode further west, traverses a prominent valley through the use of terraces cut into the hill-side. Similarly it uses terraces across the contours to cross a deeply incised stream east of Asthall Leigh at Pool's Bottom. Its crossing of the Windrush may have been by bridge as a stone abutment can be seen in a marshy area alongside the river. The crossing of the Evenlode is difficult to detect as the river's course has been altered with the building of the Oxford-Worcester railway. Elsewhere, it appears that paved fords were used to cross streams.

The construction of Akeman Street does not conform to the popular notion of a Roman road with paved surface and side ditches on its course through the Wychwood area. It has been sectioned in a number of places between Blenheim Park and Asthall with the conclusions that its width is not constant and the method of construction varies with locally available materials. During March 1940 a short length of the road was sectioned at several places at Chasefield Farm between Ramsden and Minster Lovell. At one point it was 16.5 feet (5m) wide and had a foundation of small slabs laid horizontally, one course thick at the edges and rising to three courses at the crown of the road. Above this was a top-dressing of small pebbles which had spread beyond the edge of the paving. This metalling was bound together with a stiff sandy clay that occurred in the natural subsoil not far away. Close by, another excavated section demonstrated the road was 25 feet (7.6m) in width with foundations of stiff, yellow, sandy clay on which was laid a single course of small limestone slabs. Above this was a top dressing of small pebbles over the crown of the road only. At neither location was any trace of side ditches found.

At Asthall Leigh sections across Akeman Street identified a width of 10 feet (3m) while near North Lodge in Blenheim Park it was seen to be 17 feet (5.18m) wide, but with small side ditches. Side ditches between 2 and 3 metres (6.5 and 9.8 m) wide and 1 metre (3 ft) deep were located where the road enters Blenheim Park in 1980. This variation in width is not only evident in the Wychwood area. To the north east at Tackley Park the excavated road was 12 feet (3.6m) wide and near Alchester 19 feet (5.79 m) wide. South-west of the Wychwood area and closer to Cirencester at Quenington it comprised a dual carriageway with a shallow but wide gutter between the carriageways, the whole being 31 feet (9.4m) wide.

On present evidence it seems that Akeman Street was not only constructed from materials accessed very locally – at Wilcote and north-east of Asthall pits have been found flanking the road which no doubt provided the construction materials – but also using local expertise which would have varied considerably too. The variations of the width may be related to the migration of the road later-ally as it was repaired through time. Presumably the maintenance of the road was also a local responsibility and there may have been a reluctance to spend resources on it especially in a rural area mid-way between two towns. Interestingly, at Quenington Akeman Street has a more sophisticated form and also near Alchester it was made up of limestone slabs laid horizontally and 12-14 inches (30-35 cm) thick, though in no apparent order. Both these instances might reflect greater use and greater wealth locally. Although the road may have been important strategically in the early years of the Roman period, the quality of its maintenance after that time might lead to the conclusion that it was used as more of a local road than a major cross country route.

Our knowledge of subsidiary roads joining Akeman Street in the Wychwood area is vary scanty although they would have been necessary. It is possible to use present metalled roads from villas, for example from Fawler to Akeman Street, to postulate the course of probably un-metalled tracks in the Roman period. One

8.1 The terraced Akeman Street at Bagg's Bottom, Stonesfield. (Author)

very startling alignment is that of St John's Lane/Pay Lane which runs dead straight from North Leigh Lane near Shakenoak, cuts Akeman Street at New Found Out Farm where both roads would have exited the Grim's Ditch, and continues towards Leafield, its line possibly being extended towards Shipton-under-Wychwood.

Certainly, the countryside would have been criss-crossed by a network of routes, some fossilised in present rights of way, but others now completely abandoned. The footpath between Ditchley villa and Stonesfield which becomes the metalled Stonesfield Riding may follow the course of a Roman track, and another footpath between Fawler and the B4437, the Charlbury–Woodstock road, would, if continued, approach the shrine at Lee's Rest. There is a clear indication that the track between Akeman Street and Shakenoak is perpetuated in the footpath through Holly Grove, and traces of it were found during excavations at Wilcote in 2000. However roads and tracks are very difficult to date before the era of maps as they rarely provide artefactual evidence, and so the search for such 'Roman' routes must remain a highly speculative, if still attractive, pastime.

Life along Akeman Street

Any discussion of the importance of settlement along Akeman Street must consider the two urban areas on its route outside the Wychwood area as these would have played a role in the trade and social networks within the region.

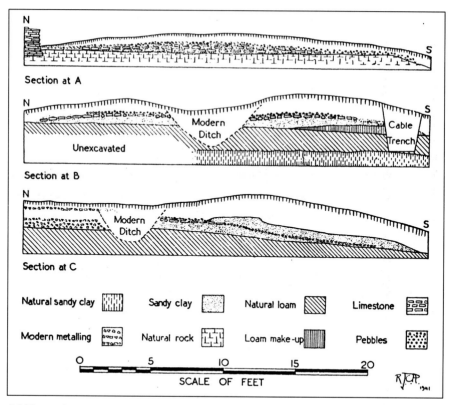

8.2 Plan and section of Akeman Street at Crawley (OAHS : *Oxoniensia* 7,110).

Alchester

Alchester lies north-east of Wychwood at the junction of east-west Akeman Street and the north-south Towcester to Dorchester road. As discussed above, the location was important as a military focus with its forts and the siting of a cross-roads was probably a key element in this strategic decision. It is likely that the first civil settlement was a vicus, a collection of buildings offering services to the troops and where perhaps the common law wives and children of the soldiers lived. As the army moved on, the settlement had probably developed a momentum as a trading centre and this formed the nucleus of the early town.

Alchester shows signs of a formal grid and was by far the largest town in the region, though probably in the *civitas* of the Catuvellauni. In the second century it was provided with defences, though probably for status reasons rather than to deter aggression, and this indicates that it must have had official and adminis-trative status. The town extended over a total area of about 43 hectares (106 acres) although the defences enclosed only 10.5 hectares (26 acres). It included a large courtyard building in the centre of the town and a number of stone buildings and so contained the most substantial structures of any town in the Thames Valley. However, no large public buildings have yet been identified and its status is likely to have been that of a market town and a major regional centre. Finds such as statuettes, painted wall plaster and mosaic pavements indicate that it was a prosperous settlement and some of this prosperity might have been due to its proximity to the villas of the Wychwood region.

Cirencester

Cirencester, Roman Corinium Dobunnorum, lies on the eastern dip slope of the Cotswold Hills. It was the '*civitas* capital', the administrative and political centre of the Dobunni, whose territory extended over the modern counties of Gloucestershire, (West) Oxfordshire, (North) Wiltshire, Worcester and Herefordshire. The building of an early Roman fort and the construction of the principal public buildings and developed street grid probably occurred three or four decades either side of AD 100. Its largest buildings would have been the basilica and forum. The basilica would have been the central place for the Dobunni as well as for the town itself, and its status was heralded by sumptuous decoration of Purbeck and Italian marble wall veneers. The forum immediately in front of the basilica was a piazza surrounded on at least two sides by ranges of rooms with internal and external verandas, and probably used as a market place. Another market place, later to have what is thought to be a meat market, a *macellum*, built on it, was probably the focus for the trading of livestock. In the north west corner of the town was a possible theatre. Shops have been discovered in the central area. The town was walled with possible towers around it and at least four gates, but present evidence suggests that not all the space was used by housing. Many of the domestic structures that have been identified indicate a variety from rich town houses around a courtyard with mosaics and wall paintings to simple linear houses. The public baths have yet to be found though they certainly would have existed, probably south-west of the forum. No temples have been located for certain, but finds of sculptural material suggest that there were temples to the Matres, the Mother Goddesses, Mercury and Minerva. It is possible that Corinium became the capital of a newly created province of Britain, Britannia Prima, in the early 4th century. This would have entailed the building of a governor's palace and accommodation for accompanying bureaucrats and guards. A church for the metropolitan bishop of Britannia Prima may also be expected. Outside the walls were an amphitheatre, cemeteries and quarries for stone and gravel for the town.

The influence on Wychwood of Corinium is hard to gauge. Certainly it would have been important in terms of administration and tax collecting, and perhaps the owners of some of the larger villas may also have had town houses there. Presumably, at a distance of 30 miles from the centre of Wychwood, its influence on trade might have been weak but much of the money earned from that trade might have been invested in the town by the villa owners.

Small towns

In the Wychwood area there are at least three settlements which might be described as 'roadside' or even small towns: Sansom's Platt, 12.1 km (7.5 miles) from Alchester, Wilcote, 8 km (5 miles) further south-west, and Asthall, 16.5 km (10.2 miles) from Wilcote. All lay close to or on river crossings. Such roadside settlements are common along the major Roman roads of southern and midland England.

Sansom's Platt   (SP 4523 1889 to SP 4535 1898)

The site of this small town lies just south of Akeman Street about half a kilometre to the east of the River Glyme and three hundred metres (981 ft) west of the River Cherwell. It is about 90m (295 ft) above sea level and on a west facing slope between two river valleys.

Roman material, pottery, brooches and coins have been recovered from the vicinity since 1894 and could be dated from the 1st to 4th centuries AD. The first excavation on the site was as a result of a survey for a gas pipeline constructed from Charlbury to Arncott in 1972. The excavation recorded the remains of a stone building which was thought to be a villa. At least three rooms were observed, including one with painted wall plaster and a red concrete floor. A further building to the east had a pitched stone floor. Finds including pottery, coins and bronze working implements suggested that the site was in existence from the first to the early fourth century. Below the villa buildings were features that were dated to the 1st and 2nd centuries AD. Close by, a Roman stone-lined pit and other pits with Roman inhumations, pottery and charcoal were also found. Sometime later a Roman building was found in the vicinity of Sansom's Platt Farm, a short distance to the north-west.

In September 1997 the Aerial Survey section of the Royal Commission on Historic Monuments (England) undertook a photographic transcription of the site based on aerial photos taken in June 1966. The survey identified a possible small town or roadside settlement flanking a probably metalled road which branched off Akeman Street. The foundations of a possible circular building were visible at the east end of the settlement. Two concentric circles within a rectilinear enclosure were interpreted as a possible temple. This feature was inserted in between the fork of two roads and may therefore be a later addition. Buildings were identified on the north and south sides of the road. Room divisions were observed in a large building. Further groups of buildings were identified to the north-west of the road. Enclosures were seen in this area and a possible east wing of a villa to

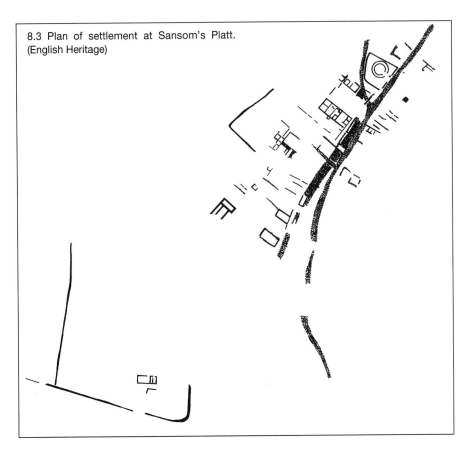

8.3 Plan of settlement at Sansom's Platt.
(English Heritage)

the west of the settlement was also identified. Further to the west two more possible buildings were postulated both within a large ditched enclosure.

The survey concluded that the features were probably a roadside settlement. Considering the possible presence of a temple and the metalling of the road, the site might even be regarded as a small town. The postulated villa could not be related easily to the settlement or to a substantial villa to the north and may perhaps be a *mansio*, an official inn related to the Imperial Post and offering shelter to riders.

Wilcote   (SP 365 155)

The roadside settlement at Wilcote is sited about 2 kilometres south-west of the crossing of the Evenlode by Akeman Street. The limited excavations alongside the road itself suggest that the occupation was confined to a relatively narrow zone little more than 30 m (98.4 ft) wide on each side of Akeman Street and at its most intense from the conquest period until the first half of the second century and then was sporadic until the first half of the fourth century. Occupation seems to have ceased about 360. However, there were signs of fourth-century occupa-

tion under the village of Ramsden and much of the area was unavailable for field-walking or excavation. In his initial campaigns (1990-92) Hands identified a large number of quarries and possible evidence for four slightly constructed timber houses. He interpreted the quarries as the source of materials for building and maintaining Akeman Street. Later occupation might have been in the form of smallholdings where some produce was grown but the main occupation of the population would have been working at the local villas. Such a 'village' might not have been very large, just a few families. Finds do not indicate military presence, though Hands interpreted the earliest phase as a military staging post, typical of long-distance trade.

If the site itself was rather inferior to the later villas in the area, the finds from the early period were of high quality. Abundant early first-century coins, Samian ware and amphorae indicated a high standard of living. Although Hands suggests that these finds reflect travellers on the road staying in primitive conditions, it is more likely that they are the result of an official presence of some sort or perhaps a high-standing local personage, perhaps connected with trading within the Grim's Ditch, as it is difficult to conceive that such a wealth of material would have been left by transient travellers. Excavation by the Cotswold Archaeological Trust in 2000 identified a spread of light industrial sites for metal working.

Asthall   (SP 290 113)

The Roman settlement at Asthall was sited south-east of the present village. Excavation was carried out in 1921 and 1922, 1947 and more recently in 1992. The site is midway between Alchester and Cirencester and on the crossing point by Akeman Street of the Windrush. The settlement may have originated from military activity in the form of a possible fort on Akeman Street, but equally the combination of an important road locally and the rich farmland around may have determined the settlement's role as a service or market centre. Aerial photographs and excavation have demonstrated that the layout of the settlement was well developed with a number of streets running north-south on either side of Akeman Street, with at least two crossroads within the settlement and an east-west 'loop' road linking them south of Akeman Street. The road pattern is skewed away from the direction of Akeman Street with no right-angled junctions. The cause of this phenomenon is unknown; it is conceivable that it represents the plan of an early fort later developed as the streets of the rural settlement, though there is no evidence for this. The settlement limits are uncertain though a minimum of 500 metres along the road is known at present. Buildings fronted both sides of Akeman Street and also the side roads with the greatest density of settlement

Opposite: 8.4 Akeman Street in Blenheim Park (Author)

being to the south-east. The earliest structures appear to have been timber-built in the late first/early second century and mainly of strip plan. Buildings were constructed on stone foundations from the mid-second century and occupation has been attested until at least the fourth century. Stone for the walls and roofs was obtained locally. Within the settlement a circular feature identified from aerial photos may represent a shrine. To the south of Akeman Street at the limits of the settlement was a fourth-century cemetery.

The evidence for the economy of the settlement is better than for Wilcote or Sansom's Platt but still rather fragmentary. Ironsmithing took place on the southern margins of the settlement from the mid-first century until the early third century and there is some evidence of small scale copper alloy working and silver refining. There is some evidence for baking and animal bone exhibits some traces of butchery. It is possible that the site was also important in the trading of pottery. The finding of oyster shells is indicative of a high status rural settlement.

The relatively developed plan of the settlement, the variety of economic activities and its size indicates that Asthall should be described as a small town rather than a roadside settlement such as Wilcote and Samson's Platt. It was clearly the most important settlement between Alchester and Corinium.

Other settlements

It is likely that Akeman Street attracted other settlements. One might have been where Akeman Street enters the Grim's Ditch in Blenheim Park. A large scatter of pottery and building materials were found when fieldwalking in advance of planning for the Woodstock by-pass, and previous finds of coins have been noted. The site, above the Glyme and behind the Grim's Ditch earthwork, might have been suitable for another small town acting as a market centre and could explain the poor development of Wilcote and Samson's Platt.

Conclusion

Along Akeman Street within the Wychwood region it would appear that the most prosperous local centre was Asthall which flourished from its relationship with a rich agricultural hinterland. Although there is a greater density of villas around Wilcote, this settlement never developed beyond its first-century role, possibly as an important trading centre within Grim's Ditch, and perhaps this was due to the proximity of Alchester and its markets. Sansom's Platt may have grown because of the presence of a *mansio* in it and does not seem to have developed beyond a simple roadside settlement. No doubt there are other rural settlements to be identified in the Wychwood area away from Akeman Street and perhaps the most enigmatic at present is that at Glyme Farm near Chipping Norton.

9

The Villas and Non-Villa Settlements

The rural settlement pattern

It has been estimated that the population of Roman Britain in the first half of the 4th century, the time of optimum economic activity, was about 3.6 million people. Of this total 125,000 (3.4%) were the army and its dependants, 240,000 (6.5%) lived in urban settlements while about 3,300,000 (90%) formed the rural population. These statistics indicate that the vast majority of the population lived in the countryside away from the towns and smaller urban settlements. The figures surprise because the popular perception of Roman Britain is of a military or town-based society, even though it was to be not until the 19th century that the majority of people actually lived in urban areas.

Within the Wychwood area, Akeman Street was a major determinant of road-side settlement location, but the smallness of these centres of occupation indicate that the vast majority of the people would have lived in villa and non-villa settlements related to agriculture. The area has at least two hundred recorded find spots of Roman material, many of which may indicate rural settlement sites. However, caution is necessary as many of the isolated finds may be related to the practice of mixing broken cultural materials with manure and distributing them across the landscape during the treatment of farmland. However, by identifying building materials, substantial spreads of pottery and, to a lesser extent, coins, it becomes possible to be more certain of the location of settlement and to attempt to ascertain the underlying reasons for its positioning in the landscape. The following analysis uses the river valleys of the area as a structure from which to describe settlement patterns.

The Windrush valley

Above Witney, where the Windrush enters the Wychwood area, evidence for settlement is found around the Hall, alongside the river, at Minster Lovell, with a villa a short distance upstream east of Worsham. Further up the valley at least one villa has been located west of Asthall, and another at Widford. Burford has produced evidence of coins, and around the present church at Taynton both coins and pottery have been retrieved. At least one settlement is sited in the tributary valley of the Evenlode at Fordwells, the name indicating an active stream and spring that is still an important part of the hamlet today. The site has produced hypocaust tile as well as pottery and building materials that indicate a structure of some pretension.

The Evenlode valley

The Evenlode enters the Wychwood area north of Long Hanborough and along both valley sides copious evidence of occupation in Roman times has been located.

On the southern valley sides at Church Hanborough and Long Hanborough pottery and other finds indicate two settlements on the spring line. At North Leigh are the preserved remains of a sumptuous villa, one of the largest in Britain. The tributary stream joining the Evenlode north of North Leigh (its Celtic name may have been Yccen) has at least two villas situated close to it, at Shakenoak and Bridewell Farms. Further to the west Roman pottery has been found at two locations within Wychwood Forest above an entrenched tributary of the Evenlode. Above Charlbury railway station extensive spreads of pottery have been retrieved and a scatter of Roman pottery also has been found at Stag's Plain, both locations being on the present edge of Wychwood Forest. A villa appears to be sited on the water-holding clays at Brize Lodge, west of Ramsden. Beyond Charlbury, the southern slope of the Evenlode valley is more open and heavily cultivated resulting in a number of sites having been identified. These are strung out along the 120 m (394 ft) contour which corresponds to the local spring line. There are indications of villas at Chilson, Ascott-under-Wychwood, south-west of Shipton-under-Wychwood and at Upper Milton.

On the northern slopes of the Evenlode a similar pattern can be perceived. The tributary stream, the Sarsbrook, draining in a south-westerly direction from Chipping Norton to Kingham, forms a wide valley which has evidence for a Romano-British farm on its western side and a small villa on the eastern slopes as well as what appears to be a sizeable settlement at Chipping Norton. Each settlement is situated in relation to a spring-line water supply. There is evidence of occupation north-east of Shipton and north-west of Ascott about 130m above OD, as well as indications of settlement activity at both Chadlington and Spelsbury. A Roman brooch found in Charlbury churchyard above the Evenlode may indicate a settlement site there also. Above Charlbury two scatters of pottery are related to springs, and at Fawler there is a villa which seems to have had a bath-house close to the river. A bank and a ditched enclosure is visible on aerial photographs at Oaklands Farm above Fawler. Alongside Akeman Street, east of Stonesfield, is the site of another very large villa structure. Roman coins have been found in at least two spring-line locations above Combe.

The Glyme valley

The Glyme valley has little identified Roman settlement largely due to its wooded nature, but a lack of fieldwork is probably also a significant factor. There are indications of a farmstead above the river at Glympton and finds of pottery at Hensington near Old Woodstock indicate scattered settlement also. It is likely that a villa of some pretension existed in Blenheim Park on the site of the medieval manor house. Ley's Farm, above the tributary of the Glyme that reaches into Heythrop Park, has produced evidence of a considerable settlement. The most densely populated area of Wychwood in Roman times appears to be on the plateau around Ditchley and Kiddington. A high density of villa structures, many less than a kilometre apart, have been located including those at Callow Hill and the well known Ditchley villa. The two tributaries of the Glyme that drain the plateau are clearly important in the location of villa sites.

The Dorn valley

The River Dorn which forms the eastern boundary of the area, has evidence of settlement in the form of coins and pottery at two points on its course, Sandford St. Martin and Steeple Barton, while the Great Tew villa, near a spring at the headwaters of the Dorn, and another on a tributary at Wootton Down again show the importance of water to life in the area in the Roman period. At Duns Tew, on a tributary stream of the Dorn, Roman coins have been found.

This evidence overwhelmingly indicates that Roman settlements were sited either in the valleys of the rivers and large streams that cross the area, or on the spring line where the clays meet the Oolitic limestones. In an area largely of limestone the major determinant for settlement siting was the availability of water for human and animal consumption. From the distribution of Roman material, it would appear that the watersheds between these rivers, often referred to as 'downs', were used for summer pasture leaving little evidence of permanent settlement.

The villas

Villas are substantial rural houses built in the Roman tradition, and indicate the aspirations of those who owned land to show their status in buildings. Villas used Roman architectural styles and decoration and were often complex arrays of interconnected rectangular rooms which were given architectural unity by the addition of a façade or portico in the classical tradition. It has been pointed out by Peter Salway that the valleys of the Windrush, Evenlode and Glyme are 'thick with villas'. However, there are a number of problems associated with the identification of villas and their functions. Of the many rural sites identified from the Roman period in the Wychwood area, Paul Booth – using the criteria of architectural pretension (for example an element of Roman planning or artefacts such as hypocaust flue tile or tesserae from mosaics) – identified 17 villa sites within a ten-mile radius of Wilcote. He also undertook a statistical exercise comparing the number of a villas in a band 30 km (18.6 miles) deep running east-west from Cirencester to Alchester. He identified two main concentrations of villas, one around Asthall and the other around Wilcote. The Wychwood area would have had much to commend it to the villa owner: very pleasing upland valleys, each close to the congenial company of his neighbours, in good sporting country, and conveniently sited adjacent to the fast road to the small town of Alchester, ten miles or so in one direction, and the city of Cirencester around thirty in the other.

However, at only a very few sites (North Leigh, Shakenoak and Ditchley) are we confident that we have coherent plans of the villas, and these three sites differed in function greatly if the extent of their buildings is taken into account. North Leigh is palatial whereas Ditchley has provided only slight evidence of mosaic pavements or baths and none of a hypocaust system. Both Ditchley and Shakenoak were little more than small cottages in their earliest form. There are also variations in our knowledge of the structures and life within the villas since the only recent excavation was at Shakenoak in the 1960s; the Stonesfield villa, which appears to have been North Leigh's equal, has little remaining evidence either in print, on site or in museums, and the Ditchley villa was excavated in the 1930s when techniques were not as advanced as today. Even North Leigh, visited by so many people each year, has seen only a little recent excavation and that was mainly concerned with removing 18th-century structures and consolidating the villa foundations for public viewing.

Villas tells us about how wealth was expended but not how it was produced. It is impossible to ascertain, on present evidence, the amount of land owned by these villas and attempts to do so for villas such as Ditchley, Callow Hill and Shakenoak using medieval or modern features in the landscape are fraught with problems. It is possible that many of the villa owners also had land in the Thames valley to help them support their establishments in Wychwood, or had commercial concerns in the region's towns. Making generalisations about such varied establishments is difficult, but it is unlikely that trade within the Wychwood area would have generated enough wealth to sustain and support establishments such as North Leigh or Shakenoak. Internal trade with the population of local small towns would have absorbed some of the surplus agricultural production of the countryside which would have been exchanged for goods and services provided by settlements such as Sansom's Platt, Wilcote and Asthall. Certainly, some of the produce would have been levied as tax, perhaps directed at the large standing army of the province of Britannia. Much of the rest would have had to be transported further afield to Alchester perhaps, or south to the large pottery industry in the Oxford area. Many of the important rural industries may have been based on the extraction of building stone from villa estates and this could well have been significant economically. Stonesfield slate has been found as far away as Silchester and possible Verulamium (St. Albans). Taynton Stone occurs in Colchester and Oolite for architectural detail occurs in the south-east of England. Considering the transport possibilities offered by the Thames, the Cotswolds is a likely source.

The excavated villas

Villa structures have been excavated at a number of locations in Wychwood, but the usefulness of both the evidence recovered and its interpretation is a function of the period in which the work was executed and the existence of coherent records.

Callow Hill   (SP 412195)

The villa straddles the B4437 on the road from Charlbury to Woodstock and is set in an enclosure about 420 ft (128m) from north to south and c.660 ft (192m) from west to east. It lies close to elements of Grim's Ditch and a small Iron Age settlement of which it may be the successor. It was known to Warton who described it as a Roman encampment and Lane-Fox recognised it in 1868 as the site of a villa, describing it as 'the remains of a rectangular enclosure thickly strewed with Roman tiles and pottery'. In 1916 a floor 'partly painted in red, green and black' about 4 or 5 yards (3.5-4.5m) square was broken with a pick, when foundations and coloured plaster were also found. The villa enclosure with an internal well was identified by Allen from the air in 1933-6 in a series of oblique photographs and in 1939 it was reported in the *Victoria County History* that the house site could be seen distinctly when the crop was off and potsherds and tesserae from a mosaic could be collected. Thomas, in 1950, trenched the villa enclosure, finding a surrounding ditch which was flat-bottomed and vertical sided, which he interpreted as being for defence, and post holes for a gate. Thomas suggested that the ditch had been cut in the second half of the first century AD and that the villa may have been rebuilt in stone in the early second century. He surmised from the pottery retrieved that the site had been occupied until the end of the Roman period. Today, ploughing has destroyed any evidence for the villa, and made any further work unprofitable.

Ditchley   (SP 399201)

Ditchley Roman Villa is idyllically placed facing southwards on the side of an intermittent stream that has no name, but indicates the importance of water in a limestone landscape. In times of heavy rainfall a spring issues violently from the small valley alongside the villa. The valley below is contrarily either a sodden water meadow or bone dry. Snaking up the opposite side of the slope is a tree-tunnelled footpath which can be traced as far as Stonesfield, and was most probably the main route into the villa in Roman times.

The site, often called Devil's Pool or Watts Well villa, was first mentioned by Jordan in 1857 as producing broken brick or tile and pottery. In 1868 Lane-Fox uncovered a pavement at the site. In 1934 Allen took the now famous air photos of the villa demonstrating that its foundations were complete. An excavation was undertaken in 1935 by C. A. R. Radford who unearthed a small dwelling house with a corridor or veranda and detached outbuildings, all standing within a walled and ditched enclosure. His technique was to clear the area of the house but only to dig long and narrow trenches across the enclosure.

Radford identified four phases in the main structure at Ditchley villa. The first house had been erected about AD 80 and was a rough timber structure, 48 ft by 32 ft (14.6m by 9.8m) and was recognised by 17 post holes, the contents of which had been removed in the further development of the house. It was likely that the walls of the structure were of wattle and daub and the excavator suggested that they carried a hipped roof of thatch and accommodated both cattle as well as humans. It was set in the upper part of a courtyard, over 300 ft (91.4m) square, enclosed by a V-shaped ditch and probably a bank formed from the upcast. An entrance in the south side was 50 ft (15.2m) wide and just within it on the west was a possible small timber-framed building.

In the early 2nd century Radford proposed that the wooden structure was succeeded by a substantial one-storied stone house some 94 ft by 49 ft (28.7m by 14.9m) with walls of locally quarried stone, resting on heavy foundations built up to the south to level the area. It was roofed with tiles and contained six rooms, with two wings projecting southwards at each end, connected by a veranda carried on wooden posts. Radford suggests that the entrance was by three steps into the eastern wing, the first room of which may have been an open portico. The portico led to the most important room which had a kitchen behind with an open central hearth. West of the kitchen may have been serving rooms and beyond them a room, the width of the building, opened onto the veranda. Two rooms which formed the westerly wing were probably private rooms. The whole design has a very classical feel to it. The walls were plastered and painted and the windows glazed. The floors probably rested on wooden joists. Shortly after its

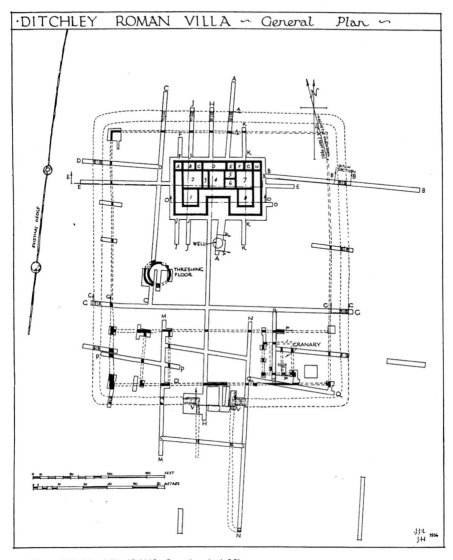

9.1 Plan of Ditchley Villa (OAHS: *Oxoniensia* 1,28).

construction a row of rooms was added to the north including a new kitchen, possible baths where water might have been thrown onto hot stones thereby producing steam, and other rooms perhaps for servants all connected by a central corridor. A well, probably timber lined and covered with a well house, was built in the centre of the courtyard and remained in use until it silted up at the end of the fourth century. West of the well was a circular structure, 30 ft (9.4m) across, with pitched foundations surrounding a cobbled area which was interpreted as a kerbed threshing floor. Across the south end of the courtyard there had been

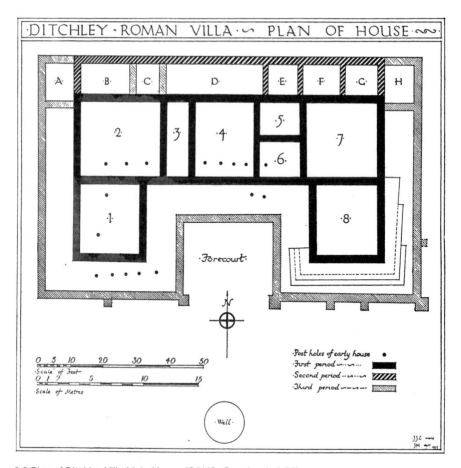

9.2 Plan of Ditchley Villa Main House (OAHS: *Oxoniensia* 1,30).

extensive outbuildings which had suffered much destruction, particularly to the west. The excavator identified a structure measuring 280 ft by 70 ft (85.3m by 21.3m) covering the west side. It was timber-framed with wattle and daub walls and roofed with thatch. It was divided at the west end by two walls and the east end contained four hearths and large quantities of pottery which were interpreted as the labourers' quarters. Traces of the cobbled floors of huts were suggested on each side of the main house except the east side which contained the main approach. There were two enclosures outside the main ditch and these probably contained orchards or gardens.

Radford surmised that the house remained in use until about 200 when a fire caused the collapse of the roof and the structure remained a ruin for a considerable time. It was later reconstructed on the same plan as previously though a new veranda was added around the front and sides. The building was roofed with Stonesfield slate and the floors were solid and finished with a mortar surface which may have carried tessellated pavements as tesserae were found. Damage to the structure made it impossible to assign functions to the various rooms. An elaborate entrance was constructed in the east wing. The identification of four stone piers carrying columns and the recovery of parts of those columns suggested that the entrance lay between two columns with arched openings on each side crowned by an ornamental cornice. There may have been a second storey reached by a staircase. Evidence of burnt floors indicated that heating was by brazier. The house was probably constructed in the first half of the 4th century and remained in use possibly into the 5th century, after which the buildings gradually became a ruin.

When the last house was built the threshing floor was reduced in size to 25 ft in diameter and the building at the southern end of the courtyard, which was in ruins, was demolished, the material burnt and buried, while on the eastern side of the entrance a small, substantial building 36 ft square was built of stone with sleeper walls. It had a raised floor and external buttresses indicating a granary.

Radford's detailed recording has enabled reconsideration of the evidence from the site, indeed it is the only villa site excavated before the 1950s in Wychwood for which the records are good enough for such a re-interpretation. Radford's results can be criticised in terms of his dating of the main house, the sequence of its development and the function of the structures identified in small trenches in the enclosure. The excavators of Shakenoak villa, Brodribb, Hands and Walker, suggested that it would have been unlikely that the villa would have been rebuilt, after abandonment for over a century, on exactly the original foundations, even though there were some additions. They also noted that many of the fourth-century finds came from within the enclosure but not from the stone-built house. They concluded that all the phases of the stone building were probably consecutive and all belonged to the second century. They suggested that Ditchley villa was a small second-century house, built on the site of a timber structure of late first-century date. The stone villa was abandoned as an independent dwelling site at the end of the second century. Occupation from then until about 370 was slight when it again became intense until well into the fifth century. This intense occupation was not associated with the stone dwelling house.

More recently Paul Booth re-assessed the excavation of Ditchley pointing out that the evidence for baths on the site was very tenuous, and that the entrance to the house was probably central and thereby reinforcing the symmetrical character. He saw the stepped foundations of the eastern wing as necessary underpinning of the structure on the sloping ground and its architectural elaboration as an enhancement of the view across the valley. Booth also considers that the 'threshing floor' may have been a round, low-status domestic or agricultural structure, symmetrically matched by another in front of the east wing. Finally, Booth considers that the southern end of the villa enclosure might have contained buildings but certainly nothing like the barracks for slaves envisaged by Radford.

Today the plan of the villa can still be seen in very dry summers when the crop is stressed, but continual ploughing must have taken its toll on the surviving remains.

Fawler   (SP 372171)

The Fawler villa lies on the banks of the River Evenlode about a mile west from the crossing by Akeman Street. The name Fawler is of Anglo-Saxon origin and is derived from *(to)fagan floram* meaning 'at the variegated or coloured floor'. The villa is sited on the north bank of the Evenlode between the village and the railway line. In 1865 a tessellated pavement with a hypocaust below it was uncovered when a land drain was dug and silver coins and pottery were also found. Another mosaic was cut through when the railway was constructed, its materials being used in the embanking of the line. Sometime shortly after 1912, a Mr Warde Fowler of Kingham identified the site and made a plan of the villa with the help of an 'aged' local inhabitant. The plan has since been lost. Warde Fowler was puzzled that the position of the pavement would have meant that it would have been submerged by the Evenlode when in flood. However, the river was diverted in the 19th century to give the railway a straight run. The parish boundary fossilises the old course, and this would have left the villa in a secure position. In 1926 a wall was opened up by the Oxford branch of the Classical Association. Silver coins and a 2nd-century Samian cup were found. From time to time coins, mostly of a late Roman date, have been found in the village and are clearly associated with the villa site.

Excavations by Oxford Archaeological Unit at the villa in 1986 established that extensive early Roman occupation, indicated by pottery of the mid or late 1st century, was evidence of the first colonisation of the site. A dog burial accompanied by a wine flagon suggested a ritual act in this early period. A first-phase building was dated to the 1st or early 2nd century, and was represented by a wall and debris which included painted wall plaster and blue-glass tesserae. Other finds from this phase, including a silvered brooch, suggested that the occupation was of high status from the outset rather than growing from modest origins. A building beside the Evenlode, probably a bath house, was dated to the 2nd century. The debris from the structure indicated that it had a hypocaust, tessellated floors, painted walls and a tufa ceiling.

A geophysical survey was undertaken by the Ancient Monuments Laboratory of the Historic Buildings and Monuments Commission for England in November 1996. The survey confirmed the presence of buried archaeological features between the village and the railway, as well as broad parallel features south of the railway embankment.

Great Tew
(SP 406277)

The villa remains are immediately north of Beaconfield Farm, about a mile south-west of the village. Plot (1705) referred to a geometrically patterned mosaic pavement having been ploughed up in the area. In May 1810 a channelled hypocaust beneath a tessellated floor, with a bath in an apse, was discovered. As a result of ditch-digging on the slope below, bones, wood ash and black earth were found '3 or 4 feet (0.9-1.2m) below the surface'. At the same time an altar was recovered to the south of the bath, another bath was found and destroyed and pottery and tiles were recovered. In 1827 a courtyard was traced surrounded by a corridor with plinths for columns standing on a tessellated pavement and a further bath building was identified.

In 1950 a two-day excavation in advance of the building of a barn disclosed yet another tessellated pavement with a hypocaust and a room with painted plaster. A year later four parallel walls running north-south were found, representing at least two periods of building, as well as one of the hypocausts damaged by debris from previous excavations and a mortar floor on which lay large quantities of painted wall plaster. Pottery from the 3rd and 4th centuries was identified although Thomas, the excavator, considered that occupation began in the late 2nd century. Further information was added in an excavation in 1966 which has never been published. Traces of a north-south corridor facing east onto a yard were observed. There were also suggestions of a similar wing with a corridor on the south side of the yard. Examination of part of the north-south wing revealed several periods of construction and occupation from the 2nd to the 4th centuries with several rooms having painted plaster walls. A hoard of 72 coins provided a date in the 3rd century for this wing. Clearly there was a courtyard house of importance at Great Tew, some of which still remains to be found.

North Leigh
(SP 397154)

The villa remains are situated close to the Evenlode about two miles north of the village of North Leigh. The villa was excavated extensively by Henry Hakewill in 1813–16 and again in 1910 by Donald Atkinson and H. G. Evelyn White who sought to explore the earlier levels of the villa illustrated, but not understood, by Hakewill. In 1956–9 Mrs H. E. O'Neil and in 1975 J. Bertram undertook further excavations to clear and consolidate the monument for public display. These were continued until 1977. However, at least two of these recent excavations have no existing records. An important event in our understanding of the villa took place in the drought of the summer of 1943, when Flight Lieutenant Riley observed from the air a pattern of marks in the pasture outside the fence enclosing the remains of the villa. These indicated the presence of buried foundations belonging to farm buildings, yards and paddocks which formed a large addition to the then known extent of the villa. Aerial photographic evidence of further buildings to the south of the south range was recorded by D. R. Wilson in 1969. A trackway could be seen approaching the east entrance from the south with possible stables, gardens and service areas on either side. Other cropmarks west of the trackway may represent early buildings.

The sequence of the villa structures has been inferred from the various excavations. However, it is complex and only a summary can be offered here (see Fig 3.3). The earliest occupation extended beneath the whole of the later south-west range of the villa. Brooches and pottery of Iron Age and early Roman types suggested the presence of a farm continuing sometime into the Roman period. Although the position of the farm has yet to be discovered, post holes and two early hearths indicate human activity.

The earliest buildings in Roman style, probably single storeyed as throughout the villa's history, were constructed either in the late 1st century or in the early second century under the walls and floors of the later north-west range. The main house and was 20.3 (66ft) long, originally containing a row of five rooms with a front, facing south, composed of a colonnaded passage between two projecting wings. At a later date the front was modified with the extension of the passage and the insertion of a mosaic pavement of a simple geometric design in red and white. South-west of the main structure was a barn possibly of aisled construction. Later a corridor or covered passage was added to the south-eastern side and red and white mosaic, similar to that in the main house, was inserted. These alterations suggest that the structure was used for domestic as well as agricultural purposes, and the similarity of alterations in both buildings indicates an attempt to make them architecturally harmonious. This was continued in the connection of both buildings by adding two new rooms between them and allowing direct access from one to the other. North-east of the main structure was a bath building, the north baths, provided with an undressing room, cool and warm rooms and a cold plunge bath. This structure has not been completely excavated. Roofing in all phases of the villa appears to be of stone.

In the next phase two wings were added to the early nucleus, a process which would subsequently, after much reconstruction, end with the complete enclosure of a large courtyard. The main rooms of the north-east wing were highly symmetrical, flanked by corridors each with a central entrance. Beyond the end of the wing was a second bath house (east baths) serving this wing. The corresponding south east wing was quite short, possibly two rooms long, and ended in a small shed or stable.

The north-west wing was completely rebuilt and fronted but a continuous corridor, dated from the mosaics as being probably early fourth century. The old

Above: 9.3 North Leigh Villa from the south-west. (Author)

Below: 9.4 North Baths, North Leigh Villa (Author)

north baths were demolished to make way for a new, more architecturally fitting set. Heating was by channelled hypocaust. As with the north-east wing the natural slope of the ground had to be terraced for building and steps were necessary at various intervals along corridors and in rooms. At the opposite end of the range was a great dining suite (now covered with a shed to protect the mosaic).

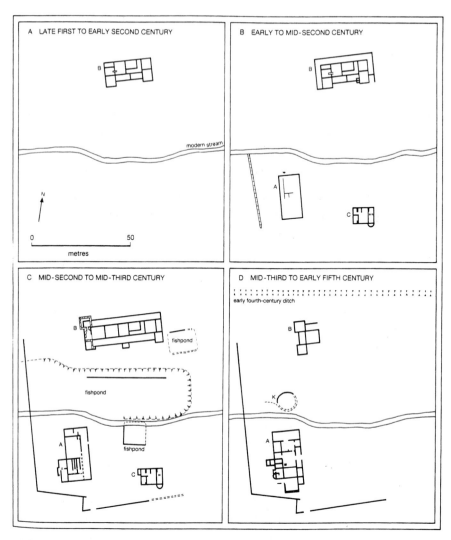

9.5 Plan of Shakenoak (based on Brodribb, Hands and Walker).

The chamber was vaulted with both walls and vault plastered and painted. The geometrical mosaic, like others at the villa, was made by Corinium craftsmen. In this phase the north-east wing was united with the East Baths which were reconstructed and enlarged. The south-west range was completely rebuilt also but was mainly composed of workshops and outbuildings including a bakehouse. A miniature set of baths was inserted into the south end of the range.

The south-east wing was not fully investigated but is known to have had a gatehouse in its centre.

North Leigh villa was clearly an important and opulent structure reaching its apogee in the 4th century when Britain seems to have been at its richest.

However, evidence for counterfeit coinage production found in the area of the north baths suggests that by the middle of the fourth century the owner tried to fill a shortage in money supply indicating how closely the villa economy was tied to the money system. Since there is probably at least the same area as yet unexamined, the villa is larger than Stonesfield and among the largest in the country. Speculation about the ownership of the villa is fruitless but the physical layout, especially the separation of the two wings for a great deal of the villa's history, might suggest divided ownership.

Shakenoak   (SP 375138)

The first published reference to the site was in the *Victoria County History* (1939) which described the presence of tiles with mortar adhering stamped with a rectangular pattern, coloured plaster and one pillar of a hypocaust on each side of a brook at Shakenoak Farm, near North Leigh village. Excavation of the site was undertaken annually from 1960–7 by Brodribb, Hands and Walker and Shakenoak remains the most complete recent villa excavation in Wychwood, though some of the excavators' conclusions have been challenged by other archaeologists. The excavators considered that occupation at Shakenoak was probably continuous from the last quarter of the 1st century AD to the middle of the 8th century. Evidence of activity before AD 70 was from a small number of objects found in later deposits and the undated remains of a circular hut.

The second century was a time of significant capital expenditure at Shakenoak and construction projects were conceived on a grand scale. A corridor house, dated between AD 70–90, lying to the north of the stream, underwent successive extensions. By the middle of the 2nd century the corridor house had simple tessellated floors, painted wall plaster and extensive use of stone pillars; a pretentious house for the period. An aisled barn, probably a granary, and dwelling for labourers, and a well appointed bath house were added to the south of the stream in the first half of the 2nd century. A series of three fish ponds, two to the north of the stream, were constructed in the same period. Later in the 2nd century the barn was replaced by a larger agricultural building.

A series of fundamental changes appeared to have occurred during the first half of the 3rd century influencing the whole villa complex. The three fishponds were filled in or allowed to silt up around 200. A circular building was constructed between the larger agricultural building and the main house in about 200 on the site of one of the disused fishponds.

This structure, which was abandoned in the middle of the century, was of a basically Iron Age form but with stone foundations. That it had been constructed on the silt of a disused fish pond and faced the facade of what had been an imposing house, suggested a lowering of living standards. The main dwelling

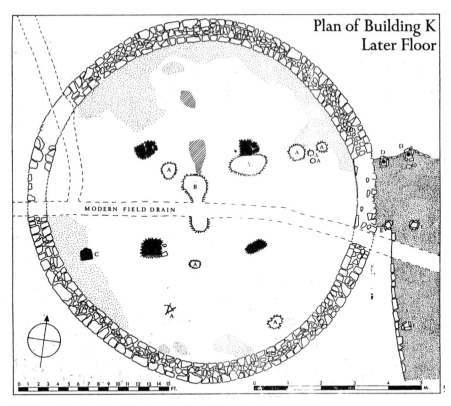

Plan of Building K
Later Floor

MODERN FIELD DRAIN

FT.

M.

9.6 Plan of circular hut at Shakenoak. (Brodribb, Hands and Walker)

house underwent changes which also indicated an alteration in the nature of the occupation and a lowering in living standards. Three hearths and a hypocaust, perhaps for a corn drier, were inserted in the former corridor of the villa, suggesting that it was converted to agricultural use and possibly accommodation for people with a lower standard of living. The structure seems not to have been refurbished and repaired as its fabric decayed. From about 300 onwards the structure was totally demolished and its site deserted except for a possible small workshop which existed in the late 4th and early 5th centuries. The former bath house was converted into an agricultural building very early in the 3rd century and it was from the debris associated with this renovation that the pottery syrinx bearing the names SATAVACUS and BELLICIA was recovered (see page viii). This structure was demolished by the middle of the 4th century. The large agricultural building was converted into a small dwelling house between 240 and 270, and underwent various modifications and extensions, including the insertion of a bath house indicating a rise in occupation standards, before ceasing to be occupied at a date around 420–430. The whole central area of the villa was enclosed by a wall in the 3rd century. Outside this central area there was a timber structure of mid-4th century date, and at the end of the 4th century an enclosure ditch was dug to the north of the site.

Stonesfield
(SP 401171)

The 'excavation' of this villa is described in Chapter Four. Its site is only approximately known today.

Worsham
(SP 306113)

The site on the north side of the River Windrush was first excavated by the Rev. G. Engleheart and Mr. E. A. Lawrence in 1908. It was further examined by Dr A. E. Peake in 1917, but no account of either intervention has been published. Peake enclosed a sketch plan of the villa in a letter to Haverfield, the Oxford professor of archaeology, and this is the main source of information on the site. It suggests that the original building was a bath house with entrance and dressing rooms and some rooms underlain with hypocausts. The thickness and depth of the wall foundations along

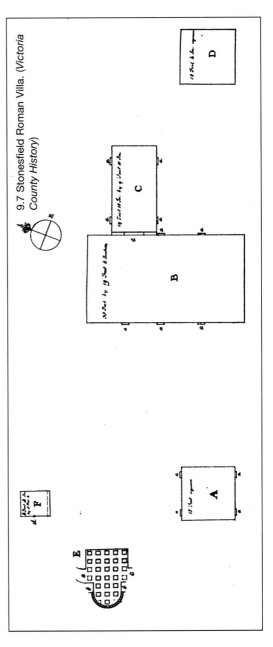

9.7 Stonesfield Roman Villa. (Victoria County History)

with the sloping of the ground to the river suggested a two-storeyed structure. In a later period the baths were enlarged and added to. In a third period of building most of the baths were filled in, flues stopped up and the floors raised, though one hypocaust may have been rebuilt at a higher level; and a series of rooms were added on the east. The new floors were of opus signinium and hard concrete and the walls were decorated with painted plaster. Pottery recovered from the site

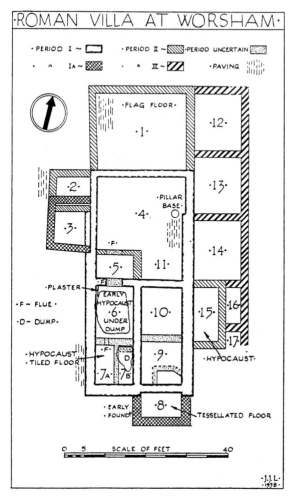

9.8 Plan of Worsham Villa. (*Victoria County History*)

dated from the 2nd century but much of it was from the 3rd and 4th centuries. The pottery and five coins recovered indicated that the period of occupation, as a bath or house, was not more than perhaps 150–180 years. The building to which the baths belonged may exist to the west at the top of the river slope.

The chronology of the villas

What in interesting about the villa distribution is the earliness of many of the structures. Ditchley, North Leigh, Shakenoak, Fawler and Callow Hill have produced artefacts of the mid–late 1st century or early 2nd century and there might be also be indications of continuity with the pre-Roman Dobunnic elite in the area with late Iron Age finds coming from some of the sites. This is more so in the case of North Leigh and Fawler where there appear to be high-status buildings from the outset. The economic and social mechanisms for this are important. Both villas have prestigious sites on the River Evenlode, the only two that we know of, and are situated close to Akeman Street. The position of Stonesfield on Akeman Street might also be significant. Perhaps we are seeing the importance of the Grim's Ditch complex interfacing with the developing Roman economy and influencing the growth of Romanised settlement types.

Evidence from Shakenoak, and to a lesser extent from Ditchley, has indicated that these villa settlements were not autonomous throughout their whole history. At Shakenoak the farm appears to have been owner occupied from its foundation around 70-80 with continued expansion of the villa buildings and increasing comfort and luxury up until the later 2nd century. However, after reaching its maximum extent around AD 180, there was evidence that the villa buildings were used for expanded agricultural purposes and to house people of a lower standard of living. A peasant hut of round shape and the abandonment of the bath-house, as well as structures not being replaced when they became in need of renovation, indicated to the excavators a change from owner-occupiership. The excavators of Shakenoak suggested this small estate was subsumed into a larger entity, in Shakenoak's case by North Leigh which has a history of expansion in the 4th century.

Ditchley also shows a similar trend. A rectangular building was constructed about AD 70 which was replaced circa 100 by the first stone building. This was later enlarged before being destroyed by fire at the end of the 3rd century. From about 200 to 300–350 the site was abandoned, and perhaps Ditchley succumbed to the growing economic influence of Stonesfield, or another site so far undiscovered, in a conflation of villa estates to produce a larger, more centralised unit. Brodribb, Hands and Walker suggest that the apparent lifting of living standards at Shakenoak about 350, and the enlarged version of the second century villa at Ditchley, offered evidence for some degree of decentralisation by the second half of the 4th century if they were to be run efficiently. This scenario, being based on evidence from the only three villas to have been completely excavated, must be treated with some caution. Even with a larger database and it would be very difficult to demonstrate such a proposal conclusively using archaeological evidence. However, it does draw our attention to a dynamic economic, and perhaps political, climate during the three hundred years of the Romanisation of the area.

Everyday life in the villa

Portraying day-to-day life at any of these establishments is impossible because we only have archaeological evidence from which to construct our picture. However, by taking Shakenoak as a case study, because the quality of the evidence is more complete than for the other villas, and complementing it with the more scanty material from other locations, it is possible to build up a fragmentary outline of everyday life.

The landscape

Evidence from seeds and timber found in the silts of the Shakenoak pond, where there was an environment protected from oxygen that causes decay, gives some indication of the landscape immediately around the villa, and perhaps further afield. However, on present evidence attempts to 'vegetate' the wider landscape, often based on soil types, can only be guesswork. The pond had water crowfoot, pondweed and fool's watercress floating on it with sages at the water's edge. On the banks were willow herb, hemlock and stinging nettle. Hedges in the vicinity of the villa appear to have been comprised of hawthorn and hazel. Evidence from snail shells around the villa suggest that there was no woodland close by. Surviving timber for the construction of the house was almost entirely oak, though some charcoal was identified as deriving from mainly from oak, hazel and hawthorn, though birch ash, beech, willow and alder were present in much smaller quantities, probably from burn hedge clippings. This is similar to the assemblage identified at Callow Hill though poplar, and holly were also found there. The presence of a considerable number of pig bones at Shakenoak indicates considerable woodland cover on the estate.

Agriculture

Villas were primarily agriculturally based establishments, although some of the wealth of larger villas such as North Leigh or Stonesfield may well have been made elsewhere. The most important factor in the use of the land that forms the villa estate is the soils that are derived from the underlying geology. Chapter 2 has indicated the physical background of the region, and as far as present evidence allows, it seems that there are no villas situated on the heavy Oxfordshire clays on the south eastern boundary of the Wychwood region. Most villas took advantage of the variety of habitats and possibilities of the both the Liassic clays and the Oolitic limestones and were sited at the junctions of these two geological systems, especially as it also formed the spring line. Each system also had characteristic agricultural uses: the Oolite is well drained and suitable for growing cereals, while the clays are more suitable for woodland which would have provided timber for fuel and building, pannage for pigs, grazing for cattle and goats, fruit growing and winter fodder for cattle.

The importance of the Oolite for cereals is seen in the provision of a granary and possible threshing floor at Ditchley and probably another granary at Callow Hill. Cereal evidence retrieved from North Leigh indicated the presence of spelt, breadwheat, barley and possibly rye, with spelt being the predominant wheat variety. The grain would have been necessary not only for human consumption but also for winter cattle feed. No evidence for fields systems has been located around the villas, though increasingly they are being identified on the uplands between the river valleys and it is likely that the Iron Age pattern of land division was maintained throughout the Roman period.

Our best evidence for other aspects of the farming regime come from Shakenoak. Sheep and goats were important there, and it was estimated that the flock of sheep was in excess of 100, possibly as much as 200 head. Sheep and goats were important for meat and wool (as a spindle whorl found at the villa implies), but also for milk and cheese. However, the high ages of the sheep, as determined by the study of bones, suggests that they were kept for breeding, wool and also milking.

At Shakenoak there was considerable evidence for cattle, mainly short-horned, but also work oxen for ploughing (no horseshoes have been found at any villa excavation in the area), reinforced by the finding of a bronze bucket ornament in the shape of the head of a short-horned bull. A byre was identified by its rough floor of mortar and stone with a gully in and was probably for the night housing of oxen and calving, while a corral of 4th century date protected cattle from wolves at night and may have been used for branding, culling and winter hand feeding as well as being a good source of agricultural dung. Evidence of the presence of bulls points to breeding of cattle. Again the ages of the cattle pointed to them being over-wintered and fed on legumes, rather than being culled during the autumn. Cattle appeared to have been raised at Shakenoak but driven elsewhere on the hoof for slaughter.

After AD 200, and the possible change of ownership of Shakenoak, it appears that beef became an increasingly important part of the agricultural regime, evidenced by the increase of beef consumption. Whilst there was evidence for grain growing after AD 200, there were no corn dryers, and as is the case at Ditchley, this might have taken place elsewhere.

The evidence from the fish pond at the villa site indicates the possibility that fish farming providing a source of food all year round, though no bones survived to indicate species. A pruning hook, probably used for fruit trees, and indications of a vegetable garden which may have produced turnips, beetroot, onions, leeks and parsnips, indicates a small market gardening economy

It has been suggested that a minimum of thirty hands were needed to manage the Shakenoak estate in the second century, two shepherds, perhaps two or three mounted hands for cattle management, two swineherds, and two ploughmen. They may lived with their families on the estate or in the small village at Wilcote on Akeman Street.

The animal bones found on site are mainly derived from the diet of animals consumed by the inhabitants. Cattle composed the largest percentage, followed by deer and horse (chopped bones were found suggesting butchery), sheep and goats and pig. Mutton consumption increased in the later 4th century and this may point to the collapse of the wool industry that depended on transportation of yarn to central weaving mills. Interestingly, there appears to have been a low consumption of pork, often thought to be an Iron Age staple. It is likely that the inhabitants of Shakenoak ate meat only at festivities and it remained a luxury throughout the Roman period. Proteins were consumed through fish, nuts, and

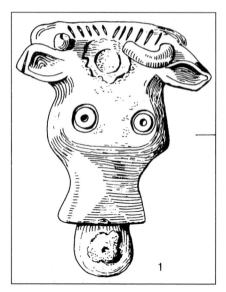

9.9: Bronze bucket ornament from Shakenoak in the form of a bull's head. (Brodribb, Hands and Walker)

milk products, while starches were acquired from cereals, vegetables and fruit. Such estimates have to be considered in the light that only a minute proportion of food waste was actually disposed of on site where it was later found.

Craft activity

The two villas that have been extensively excavated, Ditchley and Shakenoak, show very similar assemblages of artefacts, though the latter is much richer. Iron gouges, hammers, large numbers of knife blades, chisels, wedges, spikes, adze, anvils, pliers and whetstones all indicate activity in repair of the house and other farm buildings. Thimbles, needles, pin-beaters, loom weights and spindle whorls testify to more domestic work, though whether by males of females is difficult to say. The wide range and amount of pottery recovered indicates cooking and storage of food and liquids as an important aspect of everyday life.

Personal items

We can perhaps get closer to the people at the villa by examining objects used by individuals. Although no fabrics survive to indicate dress styles, hobnails, leather shoes, boot cleats and iron buckles, testify that some of the inhabitants wore shoes at least on some occasions. Bracelets made of shale, jet, wire and bronze, rings, belt decorations and chains show that these people took care of their appearance, as do glass beads, brooches, earning and pins. Personal hygiene is reflected in nail-cleaners, tweezers, bone combs, ear-scoops and unguent spoons for getting body oils out of phials. At Shakenoak an oculist's stamp gives evidence of eye problems, though otherwise disease and pain are absent from our understanding of the life experience of the villa occupants. Occasionally we can get an insight into the taste the way these people relaxed through gaming pieces, handles of tankards, or the pipe-clay figurines that may have toys but more likely religious objects. Finally, styli, thin, cylindrical pieces of bronze for writing on wax tablets remind us that at least some of the inhabitants must have been literate and numerate.

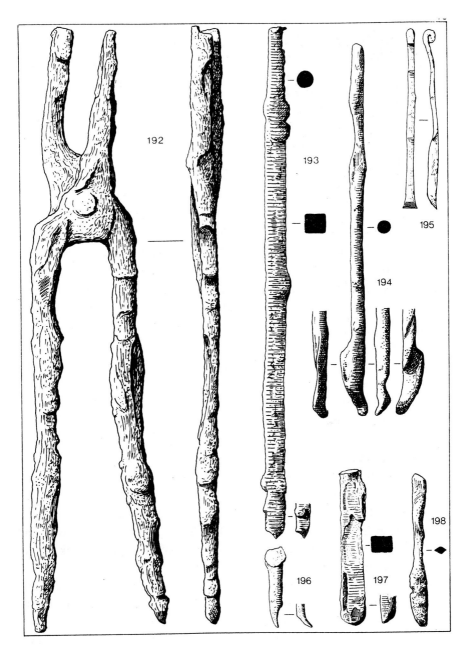

9.10 Iron pliers from Shakenoak. (Brodribb, Hands and Walker)

Non-villa settlements

As we have seen, the Wychwood area had a high density of villas in the Roman period, but these must have been served by a rural population. While rural society was probably dominated by the landowners, themselves successors

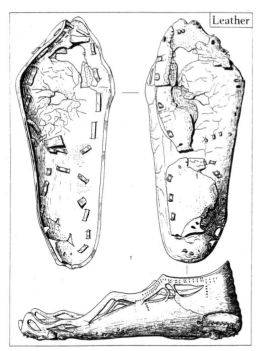

Leather

9.11 Leather shoes from Shakenoak. (Brodribb, Hands and Walker)

of the pre-Roman Iron Age tribal aristocracy increasingly Romanised over the generations, it is likely that the majority of the population in the countryside did not inhabit villa-like structures. In the 4th century, when villa life was at its fullest, there are about 1000 known villas which comprises less than 1% of estimated number of rural settlement sites. The remaining percentage of the population would have still have been working on the land and possibly living in ways little different from those of their ancestors. Our knowledge of these settlements, isolated dwellings or small villages, in very incomplete. Part of the problem is that archaeologists in the past have sought out the more easily identifiable, and richer, villas, but scatters of pottery without building materials indicating low status timber and thatch dwellings have been identified at a number of locations. We know of non-villa sites around Charlbury, above Shipton Under Wychwood and in the area of the Rollright Stones. The early phases of the Lee's Rest shrine appear from the finds to have been linked with agriculture. A number of small rectangular ditched features within the area may be structures such as barns outlying from villas or even sites half way in status between villa and non-villa settlements.

No doubt many more of these lesser settlements exist, some perhaps lying under present day villages. In other parts of Southern England where the surface geology and soils are more amenable to producing crop marks, whole landscapes of hierarchical settlement, individual dwellings, farms, villas linked by trackways and roads have been recognised and there is no reason why this should not be the case in parts of the Wychwood area.

It is likely also that in the first centuries of Roman occupation, many of these small settlements comprised of the traditional round houses, and that outside the immediate environs of villas these are still to be found. The identification of such structures has been constrained by the limits of excavation of the Wychwood

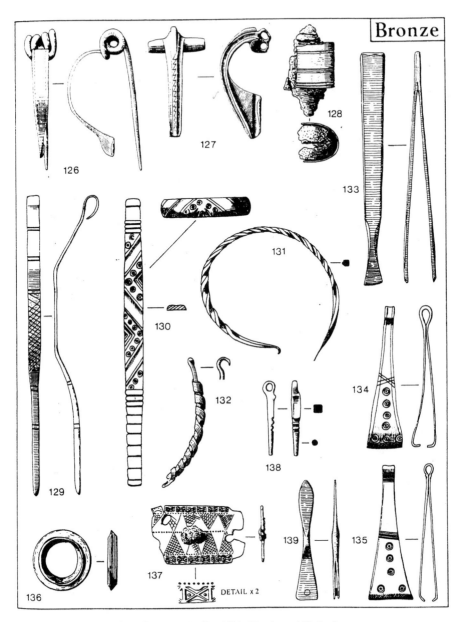

9.12 Bronze tweezers from Shakenoak. (Brodribb, Hands and Walker)

villas in the past which have been focused on recovering evidence of the main
Romanised structures. However, at Shakenoak (and possibly Ditchley) in the
third century a round house of Iron Age type was found overlying a silted up fish
pond and this may indicate that the type of dwelling existed alongside the
Roman-influenced rectangular structures of villas throughout a large part of the
Roman period.

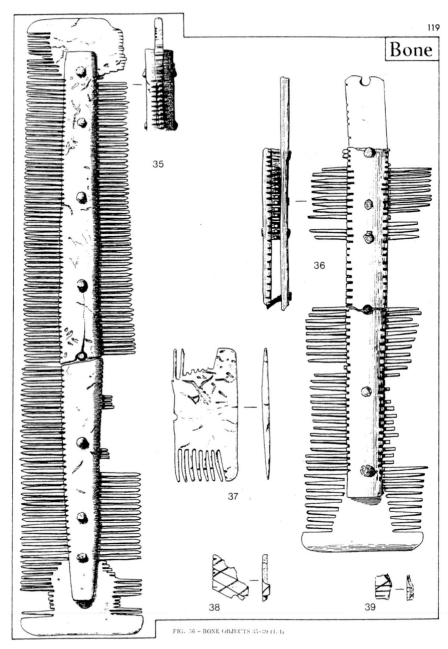

9.13 Bone comb from Shakenoak. (Brodribb, Hands and Walker)

Industrial activity

While there are indications of metalwork activities taking place at some the villas, there is little evidence for any larger industrial processes, though excavations at Wilcote in 2000 and not published at the time of writing identified large scale light industry. As has been seen above, there is evidence for copper alloy working and silver-refining at Asthall, though the source of the iron implements that have been recovered in such significant quantities at the villas probably has to be looked for outside the area, though no doubt repairs were taking place in the villas.

Two sites associated with pottery making have been discovered in the region, at Hanborough and Cassington. At Hanborough two kilns dated to the 1st century and were not associated with any settlement, though probably provided pottery to sites in the near vicinity. The two Cassington sites were either side of the late Iron Age valley fort, one of which dated to the 1st century and the other to the second, though with no evidence of continuity. It is likely that the settlement absorbed the whole output of the kilns. None of these sites would have been particularly long lived, and produced course wares for local use only using small amounts of suitable clay and whatever woodland was still surviving for fuel. There are probably many sites of this nature to be discovered in the Wychwood area, but will be difficult to find since they operated for such a short time. With the development of the massive Oxford pottery industry based on an area of 80 square kilometres east of the Thames and Cherwell, the Wychwood area was well supplied with pottery.

10

Religion in Iron Age and Roman Wychwood

Iron Age ritual and religion

We have very little evidence for Iron Age religion and ritual in the Wychwood area, though this is a common pattern repeated throughout southern England. Iron Age communities in the area practised a religion that was close to nature and would have certainly have included the veneration of natural features which were seen as connected to the divine world, and the animals and birds that inhabited the countryside. It is likely that the deities of the area had very local power and may not have been venerated elsewhere. Examples of other religious and ritual sites of this period, for example at Uley in Gloucestershire, indicate that formalised religious architecture was not required for an act of worship, though there may very well have been a boundary ditch or fence between the sacred area and the world of humans. If a shrine did exist it would have been small and acted for a focus for predominantly open air rituals linked with watery places or sylvan groves. We are aware of at least one Romano-Celtic temple in the area, Lee's Rest, where evidence for an earlier shrine may have been destroyed by later structures. Images and inscriptions are largely unknown from Iron Age religion and it is on Roman writers that we depend for much information and also on Iron Age cults surviving into the Roman period. Julius Caesar tell us that the goose, cock and hare were sacred to the Britons, but we have no evidence for this in our area. Offerings of animals, cattle, pigs, sheep, goats, cereals, fruit and alcoholic beverages or even wine were made to the deity in the hope of recompense, to reflect the creative energy of the god and the desire of the giver. Watery contexts such as rivers and streams seem important foci of worship in the Early and Late Iron Age though in a limestone region these are scarce. However, a bronze cauldron found in the river Cherwell from Shipton-on-Cherwell suggests the worship of rivers. The Lee's Rest shrine is also associated with a spring. The hillforts are likely to have remains of shrines in central positions as discovered at fully excavated sites elsewhere. The Grim's Ditch probably had several shrines as befitting a place of tribal importance, and indications of rectangular features that may well be sacred places are seen on aerial photography of the Blenheim area between the Evenlode and Glyme. Evidence of ritual shafts, dug perhaps to communicate with the other world and used for deposition, are difficult to locate, as are the sites of sacred groves which also played a part in ritual practices according to ancient classical authors.

Roman religion

When the Romans occupied Britain, they brought with them the practices of portraying deities iconographically and identifying them by name epigraphically. They also introduced the tradition of worshipping supernatural forces in sacred buildings – temples – which had a formalised religious architecture that identified them as exclusively associated with religion and ritual.

Roman religion had its own gods, calendar and festivals and the Roman army especially brought their gods with them: Jupiter, Fortuna, Mercury and other divinities originating from Italy were venerated in the Wychwood area. At the heart of Roman religion was the need to gain the co-operation of these gods, through prayer and sacrifice, and religion permeated every aspect of life. The evidence we have for religion and ritual in the Wychwood area is from two sources, possible shrines and sculpture.

Shrines

Roman religion was practised in much more imposing architectural structures which were larger than their Iron Age counterparts. In Britain, the most frequent form of temple building is the so called 'Romano-Celtic' type. This structure consisted of an inner *cella*, surrounded by a concertic portico, an ambulatory (of rectilinear, circular or polygonal shape), the whole set within a *temenos* (a sacred enclosure) which was defined by ditches or walls. This layout was very different from the classical Graeco-Roman columned temple. Usually, the temple building faced east. Often structures have been found within the sacred precinct which have been interpreted as priest's houses, shops or guest houses.

Romano-Celtic temples were built to meet the spiritual needs of the communities they served by venerating the god or spirit considered to dwell in a particular location. Temples and shrines were large enough for at least some of the worshippers to enter the building, although, as in the Iron Age, much of the ritual would have taken place in the open. Temple buildings had the very practical role of keeping birds and rain off the statue or other representation of the deity rather than providing a focus for congregational worship which took place outside. Acts of worship might include private worship, communal gatherings or healing by priests. Therefore evidence of occupation need not have been very intensive.

Romano-Celtic temple sites are rare in England with only about one hundred and fifty having being recorded, though they are more widespread in southern and eastern England than in other areas. A number of possible shrines or temples have been located within the Wychwood region. Also just outside it, at Woodeaton, was an important temple which has produced a rich collection of votive offerings which may be due to its position on the tribal boundary of the Dobunni and Catuvellauni.

Asthall

Aerial photographs of the settlement have shown a round feature that might be interpreted as a shrine. There is also the possibility of a cult site with two wells, one of which had a deliberately layered filling of ritual deposits including five complete dog skeletons, a horse jaw, complete pots, many potsherds and animal bones and a first-century brooch. A pit nearby produced pottery sherds, charcoal, bone and bronze pins and iron objects. Subsequently a miniature bronze votive axe and a bronze swan-shaped jug handle were found on site.

Blenheim Park

Near Fair Rosamund's Well is a square earthwork that has been interpreted as an enclosed Romano-Celtic temple. It is sited above the steep valley of the Glyme, landscaped to form a large artificial lake in the 18th century. It is not difficult to suggest why such a religious site was positioned in this location as it overlooks the entrenched meanders of the lower Glyme, now lake-filled. This landscape is most unexpected after the gentle gradient of the river only a few kilometres upstream. The deeply etched meanders in the Oolite give the impression that Blenheim Park was uplifted above the surrounding landscape. Walking from Ditchley Gate the path begins to rise near the Statue of Victory and then, suddenly, there is a steep, dramatic drop into the lake. On the south-western side of the park there is cliff-like slope down to the valley of the Evenlode. Geomorphologists have suggested that water flowing from shrinking glaciers at the end of the Ice Age deeply cut this, now misfit, river, whose effect is both star-tling and awe-inspiring. There is evidence for a Roman villa on the north side of the later lake, and the medieval Woodstock Palace was positioned close by. Today, Blenheim Palace, on the south lake side, uses the valley as a picturesque setting. The spectacular natural phenomenon, even after 17th and 18th century landscaping, was bound to attract specialist occupation, as it attracts so many walkers now, and it might be suspected that this was always a place of awe in a usually undulating landscape. The discovery of a shrine reinforces this concept and the siting of the temple may have been because of the scenic effect of the valley or proximity to the spring that issues at Fair Rosamund's Well.

The enclosure, which has not been excavated, survives as a ditch and bank containing an area 19m (62 ft) square. The bank measures 3.5m (11.5 ft) wide and stands up to 0.3m (1ft) high on all sides. The outer ditch is now in-filled but is still visible as a shallow depression 2.8m (9.2 ft) wide. The original entrance may be represented by a break in the south-east corner of the earthwork. Undoubtedly, the structures relating to the religious functions of the site – pits, post holes and trenches – will still survive in the interior as it is quite clear that the site has never been ploughed. A number of possible Romano-Celtic temples appear to be concentrated in the area between the River Evenlode and the River Glyme and this may be related to a possible central focus of the Grim's Ditch complex.

Lee's Rest

This is a triple-ditched enclosure, interpreted as a Romano-Celtic temple, situated 200m (654 ft) north-east of Lee's Rest Farm. The southern part of the monument can still be seen as a series of low earthworks within woodland. The remainder of the enclosure is buried. The enclosure is square with an internal area 40m (131 ft) across surrounded by three ditches which, from the inside out, measure 3m, 7m and 7.5m (9.8ft, 23 ft and 24.6 ft) across respectively. All three ditches are interrupted by a single entrance causeway which approaches the site in the middle of the enclosure's south-east facing side. These might well have defined the sacred precinct or *temenos* within which was the temple building itself. Some 20m south of the monument is a spring, often the focus of Celtic shrines.

During the excavation of the site (see Chapter 4) it became clear that its character had changed at the end of the third century. Linington postulated that a marked change in the nature of the occupation had occurred. Over a large part of the interior of the enclosure the soil and underlying clay were removed down to rock surface, thereby also removing the evidence for previous occupation. The cleared area was then filled with a layer of rammed-stone cobbling. He thought that the cobbling had come from the outer ditch which he dated to this period, and that the ditch also had an internal bank. Little evidence for structures of this period had survived modern ploughing, but some pits and gullies were identified cutting through the cobbling, and stone roofing slabs indicated the presence of a substantial building. The occupation of the cleared area appeared to continue until the middle of the fourth century when the site seems to have been abandoned.

The site was not very exciting in terms of the structures located and examined but the finds indicated that something unusual had occurred during the time of the change of use. Finds from throughout the length of occupation of the site appeared from to be mainly associated with agriculture. However, the number of small bronze objects recovered suggested a religious use and this was further

10.1 Head of Mercury from Lee's Rest. (Ashmolean Museum)

supported by the recovery of a small stone head, carved in local Oolitic limestone with indications of two stumpy wings, possibly from a statue of Mercury. In a letter written some seventeen years after the excavation, Linington also lists a child burial as coming from the site, though this was not reported in his summary. Several pottery roofing slabs, probably of third-century date, had applied heads arranged vertically down the centre of each, and this also suggested that they had been used as vertical decorative features down the slope of the roof. These may relate to the importance of the head as a focus of ritual for Iron Age and Romanised Celtic communities. Linington postulated that during the third century reconstruction of the site, in addition to the more normal farming usage, some shrine or other building with religious associations had been present on the site. In his summary report Linington suggested that this interpretation was borne out by 'some unusual aspects of the planning of the interior at this period'. However since the plans have never been published it is difficult to know what was meant by these statements. The possible dedication to Mercury, the most common of the gods worshipped by the Celts, is significant also in that he was the patron of traders and travellers and this might have some bearing on the location of the shrine so close to Akeman Street and just outside the Phase One of the Grim's Ditch.

Speculation about the presence of a Romano-Celtic at Lee's Rest has continued and some aspects of the site are intriguing. For example, the scheduling document (March 1994) suggests the finding of a 'fine bronze figurine' at the time of Linington's excavation though it is not mentioned in his notes or summary article. The remaining features identified at the site do indicate a possible religious use.

Linington interpreted the two inner ditches as both being constructed in the first century AD. He thought that only the inner ditch, which had a bank along its inner edge, appeared to have been left open, while the other one was used as the foundation of a palisade trench. The whole sequence of palisade, ditch and bank seemed to have formed a defence for structures in the enclosure none of which was identified. These structures had been destroyed by the 3rd century changes and it is possible that they represent an earlier, Iron Age shrine or temple.

Sansom's Platt

A possible circular temple has been identified from aerial photography in the angle between two roads in the Roman settlement. Circular temples are rare but examples are known from Silchester and Caerwent and may be descended from the idea of a circular hut where the deity resided.

Sculpture

Since, British temples rarely yield positive identification of a dedication, the sculpture is very important in our understanding of religion in Wychwood during the Roman period. However, it is likely that the sculpture was set up by articulate and wealthy Britons who wished to emulate Roman ways and it will therefore be largely related to the villas. It is unlikely to represent the peasants who were probably conservative and continued to worship local gods, or possibly Celto-Roman hybrid gods. Besides the possible effigy of Mercury discussed above, a number of other gods are represented in the area.

Jupiter

At Glyme Farm south-west of Chipping Norton a bearded male head, possibly of Jupiter, was found. Part of the nose was missing and the head was rather battered. The head has heavy brows, prominent lidded eyes and luxuriant beard and hair. The mouth is well cut with a pronounced depression on each side of it. The cutting is of fairly high quality. The sculpture is probably from a votive relief.

10.2 Head of Vulcan from Duns Tew. (Ashmolean Museum)

Vulcan

Vulcan was a Roman god connected with personal aggression and at Duns Tew, below ground in meadowland at front of Ilbury camp, a representation of the deity was found. The carved side was downwards and very worn with indistinct details, but the image holds a hammer in its right hand and tongs in the left. An anvil is portrayed on the left side.

Domestic religion

Fortuna

At Shakenoak a possible votive relief of Fortuna was found. It was part of an altar and the left side of the capital and the upper portion of the shaft survive. The back is undecorated but the front carries the head and the upper part of a human figure carved in fairly high relief in a shallow niche or recess with rounded top. The top part of the female figure has long hair falling down the sides of the neck and drapery passing in a thick fold over the left shoulder and apparently covering the chest. On the left side is an object that might have been part of a cornucopia brimming with fruit. Fortuna, a protector of the state and the Emperor, was particularly popular amongst civilians as well as soldiers. A common find spot is connected with bath houses were she was particularly important to defenceless, naked men and baths were always a possible fire risk with the heating of their water.

Close to the Roman villa at Stonesfield a votive relief of three domestic deities, possibly of 3rd or 4th century date, was found near Akeman Street. Part of the base was missing and it had sustained recent plough damage to the head and uppermost of the three figures making identification difficult. Carved in local Oolitic limestone the relief depicts a male and a female figure placed to the right and left of a central plinth that is surmounted by a carved bust. A column and capital can be observed on the left side, supporting a gable. The male figure is a genius or spirit of watchfulness, self-nourishment or silence, possibly Bonus Eventus, wearing a tunic and probably holding a mantle. He has a cornucopia in his left hand and a *paterna*, a round dish used for wine, from which a libation is being poured over a centrally placed altar. The female figure appears to be Ceres, Fortuna or Abundantia with her right arm folded across her body. It is uncertain whether she is holding traces of a rod/staff or rudder, an attribute of Fortuna, which extends down from the position of the right hand along the inside line of the right leg. This could equally be a drapery fold. Ceres the corn goddess was important for villa owners engaged in agricultural practices. *Genii loci*, spirits of place, were everywhere in Roman Britain and they deserved propitiation. The damaged bust might be a Lars or possibly the donor. The most important genus

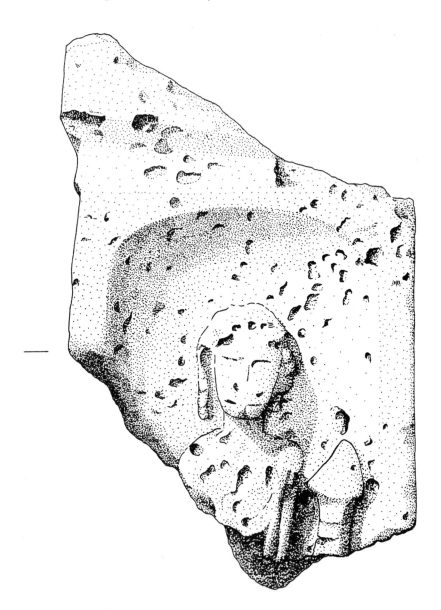

10.3 Altar of Fortuna from Shakenoak. (Brodribb, Hands, and Walker)

was the spirit who looked after the household, the Lars familiaris, whose place was in a house shrine. It is probable that all the villas had such shrines.

Fragments were found at Shakenoak of two pipeclay figures probably representing a female deity, possibly Venus. Pipeclay figurines were mass produced on the Continent and were brought as gifts to the deities to petition them for favours.

Burial ritual

In the early part of the Roman period the main method of disposal of human remains was by cremation. In spite of many excavations on villa sites we still do not know the location of their cemeteries and the only indication of funerary monuments comes from two pieces of much damaged carved stone from Shakenoak which may represent a funerary monument. It is likely that the carving features a lion.

Christianity

Inhumation burials were discovered to the south of Asthall during the 1992 excavations. The sample was very small, 11 burials, but the cemetery appears to have originated in the 3rd century with the majority of the burials in the 4th century. Paul Booth, the excavator, suggested that the change in grave orientation from north-south to west-east might indicate the adoption of Christian practice. If so this is the only evidence for Christianity in the Wychwood area during the period. Other interesting aspects of burial ritual identified at Asthall include the use of coffins and the presence of grave goods, favourite objects to be used in the after-life. One adult skeleton had a copper alloy wire anklet on its right ankle and above the body an iron brooch and iron stylus. Curiously a child burial had two dog feet to the left of the skeletal remains. This might not have any more significance than being the remnants of a dog skin buried with the child.

At Widford (SP 274121) is the small medieval church of St. Oswald, with the chancel and nave under one roof. Inside the church are the remains of a Roman mosaic, now covered up to deter souvenir hunters. It has been suggested that this might be an example of continuity of worship from a Roman 'house church' to a Saxon church, but it is more likely that the 11th century builders found a particularly attractive floor over which to place the building.

11

The End of Roman Wychwood

In AD 380 Britain was still part of the Roman Empire and the way of life of the people was as it had been for three hundred years. Fifty years later Britain was on its own, no longer part of the Empire and the Roman way of life was in pieces. Whatever happened, it happened very quickly, and was not very pleasant. It is very difficult to know what occurred in the years 380 to 430 and archaeologists still argue over the events.

The quality of excavations in Wychwood does not give us any clear evidence for the end of the Roman influence in the area or confidence in some of the interpretations of that evidence. Certainly the villas seem to have been occupied up until the early fifth century as is seen by a hoard of coins found near Ditchley villa in 1935, which was dated later than 395. No new villas were built and there were no new extensions to the villa buildings in the area, though dating of the structural changes is a problem.

We should not be looking for signs of damage by invading Saxons as the villas were probably abandoned as the economy collapsed due to lack of coinage and trade. As connections with the Roman Empire were cut, no new coins arrived in Britain. This made life in towns very difficult as trade had depended on coinage. Many industries collapsed, especially the pottery industry that was so important to the Roman way of life. Without coins, taxes could not be collected and the public buildings in towns like the baths and forum and basilica could not be maintained or roads repaired. Without the wealth of trade, houses in the towns were not repaired and collapsed and few new houses were built. In many towns thick layers of 'dark earth' have been found over the rubble of these buildings. This earth may have been made by the collapse of timber-framed buildings with clay walls. Pollen found in this dark earth has been identified as being from plants that take over waste ground. What may have happened is that large parts of towns became derelict and grasses, herbs, weeds and scrub took over them. Soon, trees also grew on the sites of decayed buildings.

The disappearance of towns was critical to the countryside. The towns had been the places were the villas' produce had been sold and this was no longer possible. The towns were also where the builders and mosaic-makers lived who might have repaired the villa buildings, but they were no longer trading. In the Wychwood area it is likely that many of the villa buildings were abandoned or fewer rooms were used. At Shakenoak it has been suggested that in the late Roman period the villa consisted of a single modest building to the south of the stream and a hut to the north. By 420 this structure is considered to have had only a single room in the north of the building in occupation. In other areas of England there is evidence that some rooms with luxurious mosaics were turned into places where industrial activities like metalworking were undertaken, and rooms that were once used for leisure were filled with rubbish. However, there is no reliable evidence for this in the Wychwood region, although 'squatter' occupation has been suggested for both North Leigh and Ditchley.

There was still a large population in Wychwood and it would still have needed to be fed and clothed. Landowners probably abandoned some of their marginal agricultural land to grassland and scrub and grew only what was needed for their own communities. The removal of the tax burden of the Roman system would have been welcome. If the villas were abandoned it is likely that the occupants joined the general rural population. That presents a problem because we know few sites where these people lived and even less about their chronology.

It is possible that Saxons were using the ruins of Shakenoak as a settlement site in the fifth century and there was probably a measure of continuity with the Saxon period, perhaps in the way the land was worked and the survival of field shapes into the medieval period. The people who were tilling the ground were probably of the same stock as SATAVACUS and BELLICIA and these less Romanised classes of rural society carried on through the ending of Roman Wychwood, just as they had on the arrival of the Romans.

If we are looking for a beginning for Wychwood it is probably about this time as the marginal land of the villas was allowed to degenerate into scrub and then woodland. By 1086 the Domesday Book records an area which is very much more wooded that at present and most likely this process began in the mid-fifth century.

12

Where to See Iron Age and Roman Wychwood

Early Iron Age

Chastleton Burrow (SP258282) A footpath cuts through this impressive uni-vallate fort without an outer ditch.

Knollbury (SP317230) Alongside the road from Chadlington to Churchill on private property. Probably an animal enclosure.

Lyneham Roundabout (SP299214) Quarried away on the south and damaged by the Burford–Chipping Norton road. The ditch and bank can be seen from the road.

Middle Iron Age

No sites of this period can be seen above ground.

Late Iron Age: Grim's Ditch

Lee Place (SP357190) A prominent bank runs through the field from in front of the road to the railway cutting.

Model Farm (SP379206 to SP384209) Walking east on the footpath it is possible to see the ditch in the woods to the south. The footpath then crosses the Grim's Ditch and turns east to run parallel with it on the west side.

Ditchley House (SP392213) Immediately east of Ditchley House the Grim's Ditch can be seen as a low bank crested by lime trees and cut by the footpath.

Blenheim Park (SP427184) The best preserved section, due to lack of ploughing. Akeman Street enters the ditch system at this point.

Glympton Assarts (SP423196) The ditch runs between two back-filled quarries. It can be seen by taking the footpath north of Woodleys.

Callow Hill (SP412195) A section of the earthwork runs downhill to the east of the footpath. To the east is the site of Callow Hill Roman villa.

North Leigh (SP380123) The only upstanding section of the earthwork easily seen south of the Evenlode. The footpath from New Yatt to the A4095 near Osney Hill Farm crosses it.

The Roman Military

Cornbury Park (SP352189) Two practice camps in the north-west corner of the Park still 'sharp' in the grass. Cornbury is open occasionally, otherwise permission can be obtained from the Estate Office.

Roads

Akeman Street (SP395166 to SP435186) At Bagg's Bottom the road is terraced into the hillside. It continues as a footpath as far as Blenheim Park and beyond as a road and footpath. The site of Stonesfield Roman villa is at SP400171.

Akeman Street (SP345145 to SP328136) New Found Out Farm where Akeman Street leaves the quarried-out Grim's Ditch. The Roman road is also crossed by another track which may be of the same age. Akeman Street can be followed on a footpath through Chasewood Farm to Riding Lane.

Meareway (SP379206) A probable pre-Roman route between Droitwich and the south-east. Now a green lane. It is respected by Grim's Ditch at this point indicating that the track is of an earlier date.

Villas

North Leigh (SP397154) Palatial villa owned by English Heritage. Partly covered in turf to protect stonework. Mosaic on view in hut. Continue on footpaths to the Evenlode and see the terraces of Akeman Street.

Ditchley (SP399201) The site of the villa can be seen by following the footpath from the Charlbury–Woodstock road, probably the main route into the villa in Roman times. On private property.

Shakenoak (SP375138) On private property but a footpath cuts through the middle of the site. It is worth following the footpaths to Bridewell Farm, site of another Roman structure, and then to Lady's Well and Wilcote Grange, returning through Holly Grove on what was probably the route to the villa from Akeman Street.

Further Reading

General

Bowden, M.(ed) (1999) *Unravelling the Past: An Inquisitive Approach to Archaeology.* Stroud: Tempus Publishing.

Blair, J. (1994) *Anglo-Saxon Oxfordshire.* Stroud: Alan Sutton.

Cunliffe, B. (1995) *Iron Age Britain.* London: Batsford-English Heritage.

Drewitt, P.L. (1999) *Field Archaeology: An Introduction.* London: UCL Press.

Henig, M. and Booth, P. (2000) *Roman Oxfordshire.* Stroud: Sutton Publishing

Millett, M. (1995) *Roman Britain.* London: Batsford-English Heritage.

Salway, P. (1993) *The Oxford Illustrated History of Roman Britain.* Oxford: Oxford University Press.

Woodward, A. (1992) *Shrines and Sacrifice.* London: Batsford-English Heritage.

Specific sites

Iron Age

GRIM'S DITCH

Copeland, T. (1988) 'The North Oxfordshire Grim's Ditch: a Fieldwork Survey.' *Oxoniensia* 53, 277-292.

Fine, D. (1976) 'An Excavation on the North Oxfordshire Grim's Ditch at North Leigh.' *Oxoniensia*, 41,12-16.

Harden D.B. (1937) 'Excavations at Grim's Dyke, North Oxfordshire.' *Oxoniensia* 2, 74-92.

Thomas, N. (1957) 'Excavations at Callow Hill.' *Oxoniensia* 22, 11-53.

HILLFORTS

Bayne, N. (1957) 'Excavations at Lyneham Camp, Lyneham, Oxon.' *Oxoniensia* 22, 1-10.

Leeds, E.T. (1931) 'Chastleton Camp, Oxfordshire, a hillfort of the early Iron Age.' *Antiq. Journ.* 11, 382-92.

OTHER SETTLEMENT

Case, H.J. (1982) 'Cassington 1950-2: Late Neolithic Pits and the Big Enclosure', in H.J. Case and A.W.R. Whitle, *Settlement Patterns in the Oxford Region: Excavations at Abingdon Causewayed Enclosure and other sites.* London: CBA Research Report 44.

Hingley, R. (1982) 'Kiddington, Tomlin's Gate.' *CBA Group 9 Newsletter* 11, 154-5.

Walker, G.T. (1995) 'A Middle Iron Age Settlement at Deer Park Road, Witney: Excavations in 1992'. *Oxoniensia* 60, 67-91.

Roman

ROADS

Atkinson, R.J.C. (1942) 'Akeman St. near Crawley, Oxon.' *Oxoniensia* 7, 109-11.

O' Neil, B.H. St.J. (1929) 'Akeman Street and the River Cherwell.' *Antiq.Journ.*IX, 1, 30-34.

Stevens, C.G. and Myers, J.N.L. (1926) 'Excavations on Akeman Street in Asthally, Oxon, February-June 1925.' *Antiq.Journ.* VI, 43-53.

MILITARY

Sauer, E.W. (2001) 'Alchester, A Claudian "Vexillation Fortress" near the Western Boundary of the Catuvellauni: New Light on the Roman Invasion of Britain'. *Archaeol. J.* 157 (2000), 1-78.

SHRINES

Linington, R.E. (1962) 'Excavations at Lee's Rest, Charlbury.' *Top Oxon.* 8

SMALL TOWNS

Booth, P.M. (1997) *Asthall, Oxfordshire: Excavations in a Roman 'Small Town', 1992.* Thames Valley Landscapes Monographs No.9. Oxford: Oxford Archaeological Unit.

Chambers, R.A. (1978) 'The Archaeolology of the Arncott to Charlbury Gas Pipeline.' *Oxoniensia* 43, 40 -45. (Sansom's Platt)

Hands, A.R. (1993) *The Romano-British Roadside Settlement at Wilcote, Oxfordshire. 1. Excavations 1990-92.* Oxford: BAR British Series 232.

Hands, A.R. (1998) *The Romano-British Roadside Settlement at Wilcote, Oxfordshire. 11. Excavations 1993-96.* Oxford: BAR British Series 265.

Winterton, H. (2001) 'A Possible Small Town at Sansom's Platt, Tackley, Oxon.' *Britannia*, 31

VILLAS

Allen, T.G. et al (1988) 'Excavations at Bury Close, Fawler, Oxon.' *Oxoniensia* 53, 293-316.

Booth, P. (2000) Ralegh Radford and the Roman Villa at Ditchley: A Review. *Oxoniensia* 64, 1999

Ellis, P. (1999) 'North Leigh Roman Villa, Oxfordshire: a report on excavations and recording in the 1970s.' *Britannia* XXX, 199-246.

Hands, A.R., Brodribb, A.C.C. and Walker, D.R. (1972-1978*) Excavations at Shakenoak I -V*. Oxford: privately printed.

Radford, A.A.R. (1936) 'The Roman Villa at Ditchley, Oxon'. *Oxoniensia* 1, 24 - 69.

Taylor, M.V. (1941) 'The Roman Tessellated Pavement at Stonesfield, Oxon.' *Oxoniensia* 6, 1-8.

Thomas, N. (1957) 'Excavations at Callow Hill.' *Oxoniensia* 22, 11-53.

Wilson, D.R. and Sherlock, D. (1980) *North Leigh Roman Villa*. London: HMSO.

Index